EXPLORING
THE
SONG OF
SOLOMON

EXPLORING
THE
SONG OF
SOLOMON

JOHN PHILLIPS

LOIZEAUX BROTHERS
Neptune, New Jersey

First Edition, July 1984

Library of Congress Cataloging in Publication Data

Phillips, John, 1927-
   Exploring the Song of Solomon.

   Includes bibliographical references.
   1. Bible.   O.T.   Song of Solomon—Commentaries.
I. Title.
BS1485.3.P45   1984   223'.907   84-7881
ISBN 0-87213-683-3

CONTENTS

INTRODUCTION

"THE SONG OF SONGS WHICH IS SOLOMON'S." Thus the book begins, a book which in some ways is the most difficult and controversial in the Old Testament. Controversy does not rage so much over the inspiration, the genuineness, or the canonicity of the book. It has been included in the Jewish Bible from very early times. Controversy is centered, rather, upon its interpretation.

God is not mentioned anywhere in this song. The book is not quoted in the Old or New Testament. Yet it takes its place confidently with the other inspired books of the Bible. The Jews read it every year at the feast of Passover just as they read the book of Ruth at Pentecost, Ecclesiastes at the feast of Tabernacles, and Esther at Purim.

Solomon calls this book "the song of songs." In the Temple there was a holy of holies; Jesus stands among men as a King of kings; in the universe there is a Heaven of heavens. And among the poetical books of the Word of God there is a song of songs.

We instinctively feel that there is more to this book than meets the eye. In some ways it is like the parables of the Lord Jesus—an earthly story with a heavenly meaning. Undoubtedly, it has a strong historical base, and is more than a mere sentimental ballad. A mere song, no matter how moving and beautiful, could not stand shoulder to shoulder with Isaiah, for instance, unless it had some spiritual truth to impart.

It is when we come to interpret this book that the discussion and debate begin. Perhaps no other book of the Bible, except the book of Revelation, has so many divergent interpretations. It is not to be hoped, therefore, that everyone will espouse the views suggested in this commentary but our interpretation is quite widely received and is by no means new.

Some see the Song of Solomon as a collection of independent poems on the theme of love. The critics who take this extreme view regard these songs as more or less erotic, and claim that they have been put together solely for their literary and poetic value. Such a view is dismissed by those who believe in the inspiration and canonicity of the sacred Scriptures.

The book has been thought to be an allegory of the history of the Jews from the time of Abraham to the advent of the Messiah; or an allegory of the emancipation of the Hebrew people from their slavery in Egypt, in the wilderness wanderings, and the eventual conquest of Canaan. Some think it depicts the relationship between Jehovah and Israel, the love of Christ for the Church, or the love of a soul for Christ.

Others view the book simply as an historical poem celebrating the marriage of Solomon with Pharaoh's daughter, or perhaps relates how he met and won the affection of a country girl.

Each of these views has its champions and it is not our purpose to explore any of them. We are going to follow a different path. Most interpretations of the Song of Solomon see only two main characters; we can see three main characters and at least four subsidiary characters. This is not a song about Solomon and a Shulamite woman. It is a song about Solomon, a Shulamite, and a shepherd. Other characters in the poem are the daughters of Jerusalem, certain Jerusalem citizens, the brothers of the Shulamite, and certain companions of the shepherd.

The story is concerned with a Shulamite shepherdess who has given her heart to a shepherd. The couple remains true to one another despite the initial opposition of the Shulamite's brothers, the combined efforts of Solomon and his court women to win over the Shulamite, and the virtual imprisonment of the Shulamite in Solomon's pavilion. Here we have allegory emerging out of history. The events recorded in the song no doubt happened. But beneath the bare historical facts of the story there lie deep, abiding, spiritual lessons.

The shepherd is a picture of Christ, that great Shepherd of the sheep. The Shulamite mirrors the Church or the individual believer devoted to Him. Solomon represents the prince of this world armed with all worldly pomp, power, and magnificence. The court women are those who admire him and who look askance at those who turn their backs upon the world, its system, and all that it has to offer in favor of an absent and, to them, unknown Beloved.

This view has its detractors. Those who oppose it say that Solomon would never thus record his own shame, but we only have to read the book of Ecclesiastes to see how fully, under the urging of the Holy Spirit, Solomon was willing to set on record his worldliness, folly, and despair.

It is difficult to see how this book can be made to fit the life of Solomon if there are only two main speakers—Solomon and the Shulamite, and if the book is a book of their mutual attraction and love. When did Solomon ever assume a shepherd character, born as he was into the royal family of David and destined as he was from the beginning for the throne?

Dr. Ironside takes the view that Solomon *disguised* himself as a shepherd for the sake of this romance. But that does not solve the problem. In the song itself Solomon is a self-confessed polygamist who has already collected sixty queens, eighty concubines, and "virgins without number" (6:8), and that, of course, was only the beginning. Before he was through, Solomon's harem included seven hundred wives and three hundred concubines. How could such a sensualist be a type of Christ and an ideal of nuptial purity? In no way is Solomon a type of Christ in the song.[1] But cast him in the role of the tempter and immediately the song takes on new meaning.

Dr. Graham Scroggie has this to say: "If we regard the king in the poem as the world, the shepherd-lover as Christ, and the Shulamite as the individual soul, we shall not fail to be helped."[2]

The story contains in every chapter, every verse, every line a deep spiritual message. Those who dislike typology and symbolism will never feel at home in the Song of Solomon for here are hidden some of "the deep things of God." I have not hesitated to explore its allegorical, symbolic, and typical teaching. I have tried to avoid fanciful, unsupported, and absurd meanings. I have not, however, drawn back from following typological truth to its logical conclusion.

Sometimes the beloved King James Version has proved obtuse in conveying the meaning of the text. I have therefore consulted and occasionally quoted from a number of other versions. In particular I have used *The Emphasized Bible, The Companion Bible,* and J. N. Darby's translation.

---

[1]No one would deny that Solomon in some parts of Scripture *is* a type of Christ. That, however, does not mean he is *always* a type of Christ.

[2]W. Graham Scroggie, *Know Your Bible, Vol. 1. Old Testament,* (London: Pickering & Inglis Ltd., Rev. Ed., 1953), page 119.

THE SONG OF SOLOMON

Outline

I. AN HOUR OF TROUBLE (1:1-8)
Introduction (1:1)
The Shulamite remembers:
A. THE FERVOR THE SHEPHERD HAD SHOWN TOWARD HER (1:2)
   Was tenderly expressed
   Was tremendously exciting
B. THE FRAGRANCE THE SHEPHERD HAD SHED UPON HER (1:3-6)
   1. She Talks About Him (1:3-4)
      The magnificence of his presence (1:3a)
      The magnetism of his personality (1:3b-4)
         Could draw others (1:3b)
         Could deliver her (1:4a)
         Could delight all (1:4b,c,d)
            Rejoicing
            Remembrance
            Righteousness
   2. She Talks About Herself (1:5-6)
      She describes herself (1:5)
      She defends herself (1:6a,b)
         Her background has been harsh
         Her brothers have been hostile
      She despises herself (1:6c)

11

The bounty of a feast (2:4-5)
　The banquet
　The banner
　The beloved

D. LOVE'S BOUNDARY (2:7)

The masculinity of the worldly women of the court (2:7a)

The modesty of the shy Shulamite from the country (2:7b)

IV. AN HOUR OF TRUTH (2:8—3:5)

A. THE LOVE OF THE SHEPHERD (2:8-14)

1. The Coming of the Shepherd (2:8-9)

   The Shulamite describes him (2:8)
   　His voice (2:8a)
   　His vigor (2:8b)
   The Shulamite discerns him (2:9)

2. The Call of the Shepherd (2:10-14)

   Volitional (to the will) to recognize a new lord (2:10)

   Logical (to the mind) to receive a new life (2:11-13)
   　The Past (2:11)
   　The Present (2:12)
   　　Beauty
   　　Bliss
   　　Blessing
   　The Prospect (2:13)

   Emotional (to the heart) to realize a new love (2:14)

B. THE LOVE OF THE SHULAMITE (2:15—3:5)

Her exhaustless bounty
Her exuberant behavior
    5. Her Perfections (4:13-15)
      She is superlatively fruitful (4:13a)
      She is superlatively fragrant (4:13b-14)
      She is superlatively fair (4:15)
  D. THE PROMISED RAPTURE OF THE SHULAMITE
    (4:16—5:1)
    1. The Shulamite's Plea (4:16)
      Her constant desire
      Her consummate desire
    2. The Shepherd's Pledge (5:1)
      His great expectation
        Marital bliss
        Millennial bliss
      His great exaltation
VII. AN HOUR OF TESTIMONY (5:2—6:3)
  A. THE DREAM OF THE BELOVED (5:2-9)
    1. A Dream of Excitement (5:2)
      A visitor who came
      A voice that called
        With propriety
        With passion
        With prospect
        With purity
        With pathos
    2. A Dream of Excuses (5:3-4)
      Her silly reasons (5:3)
        The relaxation excuse
        The ritual excuse
      Her sad reward
      Her swift remorse

I know where he is (6:2)
I know whose he is (6:3)
VIII. AN HOUR OF TESTING (6:4—8:4)
  A. Solomon's Flatteries (6:4—7:9)
    1. Solomon's Flatteries Resound (6:4-10)
      You are fair (6:4-7)
        That which is imperial (6:4)
        That which is impossible (6:5a)
        That which is impeccable (6:5b-7)
          Her glory
          Her gladness
          Her goodness
      You are first (6:8-10)
        By count (6:8)
        By contrast (6:9a)
        By confession (6:9b)
        By conquest (6:10)
    2. Solomon's Flatteries Rebuffed (6:11-13)
      The Shulamite's Explanation (6:11-12)
      The Seducer's Exclamation (6:13a)
      The Shulamite's Exasperation (6:13b)
    3. Solomon's Flatteries Resumed (7:1-9)
      His bold description of the Shulamite (7:1-5)
        Her feet (7:1a)
        Her thighs (7:1b)
        Her form (7:2-4a)
          Independent life (7:2a)
          Incomparable loveliness (7:2b)
          Infinite love (7:3)
          Invincible loyalty (7:4a)
        Her features (7:4b-5)
          Something desirable (7:4b)
          Something defiant (7:4c)

What they relished (8:6a)
   Love's seal
   Love's strength
What they realized (8:6b-7)
   The vindictiveness they expected (8:6b)
   The victory they experienced (8:7)

B. THE SHULAMITE AND HER BROTHERS (8:8-12)
   An assessment (8:8-9)
      What they perceived (8:8)
      What they proposed (8:9)
         If a wall (invincibility)—a palace
         If a door (invitation)—a prison
   An assertion (8:10-12)
      The Shulamite's testimony (8:10)
      The Shulamite's triumph (8:11-12)

C. THE SHULAMITE AND HER BETROTHED (8:13-14)
   The Shepherd's last request (8:13)
   The Shulamite's last reply (8:14)

THE BOOK AS A WHOLE

SOLOMON WAS ISRAEL'S most flamboyant and extravagant king. His wisdom was proverbial even in his own day. His enormous wealth and tireless industry are described at some length in the historical books of the Bible. He built a temple in Jerusalem which rivaled for splendor and costliness any of the seven wonders of the world. In his pursuit of knowledge he wrote, collected, edited, and published numerous proverbs and songs. In his early years he enjoyed, in an exceptional way, the rich blessings of God.

There are three main characters in this song. There is Solomon, of course, and the Shulamite, a lovely country girl who had caught the king's roving eye. The third character is the shepherd, the Shulamite's true beloved to whom she has given her heart and to whom she remains true. The real romance in the Song of Solomon centers around the mutual love of the shepherd and the Shulamite. The shepherd himself, however, remains largely in the background. He is absent, but the shepherdess loves him, longs for him, looks constantly for his coming. Solomon, in all his pomp and power, makes every effort to impress the Shulamite and to draw her affections from her beloved to himself.

Thus the allegory begins to emerge. The Shulamite represents the Church, the betrothed of Christ, or the individual believer. The shepherd pictures the Lord Jesus who has already won the believer's heart. He is absent right now although He visits us, makes Himself real to us in our moments of communion, and has promised to come again and to receive us to Himself. Solomon depicts the tempter, the enemy of our souls, who uses all the allure-ments of the world in his efforts to seduce us from our loyalty to Christ.

The book divides into nine main parts. Because of the complexity of the book's structure we will first examine the song as a whole and pick out its main movements. It will be evident that here is a song to stir the soul, to draw out the heart in fresh love for the Lord Jesus, and to alert us to how strong and subtle are the forces which would pull us away from Him.

I. AN HOUR OF TROUBLE (1:1-8)

The Shulamite has been tending her flock. Suddenly she is seized and abducted to Solomon's pavilion. She is natu-rally very much alarmed. Into the tent come sophisticated, glamorous women of Solomon's court. They are amused and disdainful, for they have overheard the Shulamite talk-ing to herself and consoling herself in love for her beloved shepherd.

"Let him kiss me with the kisses of his mouth," she says, "Thy love is better than wine." She is not talking about Solomon. He does not interest or attract her. Little does she care if Solomon's women despise her. "I am black but comely, O ye daughters of Jerusalem," she says. Then she turns her back upon them and continues to call for her absent beloved: "Where are you?"

It is a good beginning. There is trouble; circumstances

have closed in upon her. Her antidote is to fill her heart
with thoughts of her beloved. That is always an excellent
way to deal with the allurements and blandishments of the
world.

George Müller of Bristol considered it the first and most
important duty of the day to get his own soul happy in the
Lord. The world is all about us. It is like the sea, lapping
against the ship, ever probing for a crack through which
it can pour and so submerge the vessel. The answer to this
constant pressure of the world upon our souls is Christ! If
we keep our hearts singing in His love, our minds filled
with thoughts of Him, and our wills enslaved to His, then
the world will not get very far.

The Shulamite is in trouble, but she hardly notices it.
She is occupied with no man except her beloved.

II. AN HOUR OF TEMPTATION (1:9-11)

Into the pavilion comes the king—Solomon himself, in
all his glory. What a showing he makes! His entrance is
designed to sweep this simple country girl right off her
feet. "I have compared thee, O my love to a company of
horses in Pharaoh's chariots," he says. He is full of charm
and flattery. Experienced in the art of seduction, he does
not stay long this time. In his first contact with the Shulamite,
he means to impress her and plant a seed of suggestion.

Thus it is with the real prince of this world, Satan. He
is clever. He has had vast experience in alluring believers
away from their loyalty to Christ. He plants a seed, gives
a hint of forbidden delights, and the promise of more.
"You don't have to give up your work for the Lord," he
will whisper, "you don't have to stop going to church, but
just take a quick look at this. . . ."

III. AN HOUR OF TENDERNESS (1:12—2:7)

Solomon, having made his grand entrance, retired almost at once to sit down to a banquet. Doubtless he was pleased with himself. But he had reckoned without God. For while he was off indulging himself at his table, the Shulamite and her shepherd had a secret meeting, communing with one another.

"A bundle of myrrh is my well-beloved," cries the Shulamite. "Behold thou art fair my love; behold thou art fair; thou hast doves' eyes," responds the shepherd. With the instinct of love the Shulamite goes right to the heart of the relationship with her beloved. She calls him her spikenard and her myrrh. Both are aromatic and fragrant spices, connected in Scripture with death and burial. It is only when we lift all this to higher ground that its significance appears. Is it not the suffering and *death* of Christ that make him especially dear to our hearts? Do we not frequently echo James Hutton's words:

> Oh, tell us often of Thy love,
>   Of all Thy grief and pain;
> And let our hearts with joy confess
>   That thence comes all our gain.
>
> For this, oh, may we freely count
>   Whate'er we have but loss;
> The dearest object of our love
>   Compared with Thee but dross.
>   JAMES HUTTON

The Shulamite and her shepherd tell each other of their hearts' desires in terms of deepest affection and endearment.

This is what the Christian life is really all about—the love the Lord Jesus has for us and the love we have for him. With this love the world simply does not have a chance. All the way through the song we hear the still small voice of the Spirit of God: "Do you love the Lord Jesus like that?" Did we say to Him today, "You are like the apple tree among the wild trees of the wood. I sat down beneath your shadow with great delight. You brought me into your banqueting house and spread over me your banner of love"?

IV. AN HOUR OF TRUTH (2:8—3:5)

The worldly women of Solomon's court return. The shepherd has slipped away and the Shulamite now has to face afresh the allurements of the world. This attack is more subtle, for it is not Solomon himself putting forth his charms, but those who are committed to him try to persuade the Shulamite that she should give her affections to their lord. We are not told exactly what they said but evidently they sought to lure her. The Shulamite, however, fresh from a time with her beloved, is more than a match for them: "I charge you, O you daughters of Jerusalem, that you stir not up [that you do not incite, awaken, arouse][1] my passions."

The best form of defense is attack, and she begins right away to tell them about her beloved: how he first came to her in all the abundance of vigorous life, "leaping upon the mountains, bounding across the hills." She tells how he wooed her, called her to himself, desired to gaze upon her

---

[1]See The Companion Bible, "The Song of Solomon" (2:7, margin) (London: Samuel Bagster and Sons, Ltd, 1964), page 923.

face. She tells of opposition at home, how her brothers tried to hinder her love for the shepherd. They had sent her into the vineyards. She tells how she would wait for her beloved and of her meetings with him in the cool of the day. She tells how she went seeking him, how the watchmen of the city hindered her, how she found him again. "I found him," she cried, "I found him whom my soul loveth: I held him, and would not let him go" (3:4). Again she begs Solomon's women to leave her alone, particularly to cease from their efforts to awaken affection for their chosen lord.

All this speaks vividly to us. Our best defense against the approaches of the world is to talk openly and freely about the Lord Jesus. Others will soon get the message. As C. F. Weigle puts it:

I would love to tell you what I think of Jesus,
    Since I found in Him a Friend so strong and true;
I would tell you how He changed my life completely,
    He did something that no other Friend could do.

All my life was full of sin when Jesus found me,
    All my heart was full of misery and woe;
Jesus placed His strong and loving arms around me
    And He led me in the way I ought to go.

C. F. WEIGLE

Begin to talk to people about Jesus and the world's talk will soon seem tawdry and cheap, if not downright vulgar and crude.

V. AN HOUR OF TALK (3:6-11)

At this point there is a change in the song. Solomon's excursion into the country has swept up the Shulamite. Now the procession makes its way back to Jerusalem. Crowds gather to watch the splendid parade as it approaches. Various people comment on what they see, each one taken up with the pomp of the king. They know nothing at all about the Shulamite or her shepherd. Of course not! The world is always ignorant concerning Christ and His Church.

There are four speakers. The first is taken up with Solomon's *passion:* "Who is this that cometh out of the wilderness like pillars of smoke, perfumed with myrrh and frankincense, with all powders of the merchant?" Christ's "myrrh and spikenard," intended to promote the believer's pure and spiritual worship focused on His passion, is in contrast with the world's myrrh and frankincense, here coupled with "powders of the merchant" suggesting passion for sale.

The second speaker is taken up with Solomon's *power:* "Behold Solomon's litter! Sixty valiant men surround it, valiant men of Israel. They all hold swords, being expert in war." These warriors were not only to promote Solomon's interests in the world, by force if necessary, but to make sure the Shulamite did not escape. She was Solomon's prisoner.

The third speaker is occupied with Solomon's *pomp:* "King Solomon made a chariot of wood. He made the pillars of silver, the undercarriage of gold, the coverings of purple, the floor paved in a most lovely way by the daughters of Jerusalem." The world can appear very beautiful to the eye, especially to the eye that has never seen Christ.

The final speaker is entranced by Solomon's *position:* "Go forth, O ye daughters of Zion, and behold king Solomon with the crown wherewith his mother crowned him in the day of his marriage, and in the day of the gladness of his heart." He occupies the position of king. What could be more desirable than that?

VI. AN HOUR OF TRYST (4:1—5:1)

The Shulamite is now in a very difficult position. Through no fault of her own she has been trapped and outwardly compromised. Her heart is with her beloved, but the snares of the world are all about her and there seems to be no way of escape. Yet in some undescribed way the shepherd is able to break through and be with her. The Lord never leaves us alone in our hour of temptation and trial. No power can prevent the Lord from getting through to the needy hearts of those who love Him.

Throughout this section of the song the Shulamite and her shepherd exchange their vows of devotion and love. "Thou art fair, my love," says the shepherd, "thou hast doves' eyes." His beloved was "a garden enclosed," her heart bolted and barred against the flatteries and promises of the worldly prince who held her temporarily in his power.

The Shulamite says very little: "Let my beloved come into his garden, and eat its pleasant fruits," implying "all that I have is thine."

Here indeed is the way to victory over the world. Our secret source of strength is in our daily quiet time, when we open His Word and listen to His voice. Backsliding stems from a neglect of this vital time of tryst with our risen Lord. Let us make sure that we get alone with Him and say:

Speak to my soul, Lord Jesus,
  Speak now in tenderest tone;
Whisper in loving kindness,
  "Thou art not left alone."

Speak Thou in softest whispers,
  Whispers of love to me;
"Thou shalt be always conqueror,
  Thou shalt be always free."

Speak Thou to me each day, Lord,
  Always in tenderest tone;
Let me now hear Thy whisper:
  "Thou art not left alone."
                    L. L. PICKETT

VII. AN HOUR OF TESTIMONY (5:2—6:3)

The hour of tryst is soon over and the women of Solomon's court return. They comment about the Shulamite's beloved but she interrupts with a testimony of what her beloved shepherd means to her. She begins with a *dream* she once had when her beloved had come knocking on her door in the dead of night and she had been too lazy to respond. All she had done was make excuses, so he simply went away. Panic-stricken, in her dream, she rushed out in search of him and had been abused by the city watchmen who had insulted and smitten her.

The Lord Jesus will not force Himself upon us. If we are too lazy to give Him time, if we make excuses, He will quietly withdraw and leave us to ourselves. This will put us in spiritual peril, in a false position, and give the world an opportunity to do us harm. No wonder the Shulamite was troubled by her dream. It was more like a nightmare—she thought she had lost her beloved. Thankfully, it was all a dream.

Then the Shulamite puts aside her dream and gives the court women a *description* of her beloved. It is one of the most magnificent pictorial descriptions of Christ in all the Bible: "My beloved is white and ruddy, the chiefest among ten thousand. His head is as the most fine gold . . . his hands, his feet, all gold. . . . His legs—pillars of marble; his hair—wavy, black as the raven's wing; his mouth—most sweet. . . ." The description touches on ten features of the beloved. "This is my beloved," she exclaims, "this is my friend."

Even the sophisticated beauties of Solomon's court were impressed by this testimony. They asked where they could find this beloved for themselves. The Shulamite, however, suspecting their motives, gave them an evasive answer.

Do we speak with such richness, warmth, and enthusiasm about our Beloved? Do we speak so that people say to us, "How can we find this One for ourselves?" Do we have the spiritual insight and discernment to be able to tell when people are sincere or when they are not really pure in their profession of interest?

VIII. AN HOUR OF TESTING (6:4—8:4)

So far Solomon has appeared to the Shulamite but once. However, he has not gone away. Now, alarmed at the passionate outburst of the shepherdess, aware that she is becoming more and more attached to her absent shepherd, the tempter decides he must make an all-out bid for her heart.

First this section describes Solomon's *flatteries*. There is a long monologue in which Solomon tries to get the

Shulamite's attention: "Thou art fair my love, beautiful as Tirzah, comely as Jerusalem, awe-inspiring as an army with banners" (6:4). The Shulamite is wholly unimpressed. Her meeting with him was quite accidental; in no way had she been flirting with temptation. She wanted nothing better than to be left alone.

The infatuated king, determined to have his own way, continues with an embarrassing description of the Shulamite's physical charms: "You are like the view from Mahanaim."[2] Beginning with her feet, he allows his eyes to rove over her form and his tongue to pour out the grossest flatteries. Her head, her hair—so beautiful! He is held captive by her ringlets, her mouth he finds as intoxicating as wine.

We are impressed, however, by the fact that he does not touch her. Powerful as he is, he could plead and persuade but he could not force.

So it is with the prince of this world, the great enemy of our souls. The archtempter can present his propositions to our hearts, but he cannot force us to bow and bend to his will. If we go after the world or yield to the demands of the flesh it is by our own choice. In the garden of Eden the serpent could persuade Eve to take the forbidden fruit but he could not force her to eat it. In the wilderness he could urge the Lord Jesus to cast Himself down from the pinnacle of the Temple but he could not push Him down. God has drawn a line beyond which the tempter cannot go.

This hour of testing concludes with the Shulamite's *firmness*. She answers all the subtle suggestions of Solomon with just one sentence: "I am my beloved's and his desire

---

[2]See The Companion Bible, "The Song of Solomon" (6:13, margin).

is towards me." Then, ignoring Solomon altogether, she cries out for her absent one to come and take her away. Solomon was silent.

The best answer to temptation is simply to turn away from it, affirming our love for the Lord Jesus and crying out for Him to come soon. The world will be silenced. It has no weapons which can succeed against armor like that.

IX. AN HOUR OF TRIUMPH (8:5-14)

The story closes with the coming of the shepherd. The Shulamite returns home with him, leaning on his arm. His brothers subject her to cross-examination but give way before her evident triumph over the tempter. The song concludes with the shepherd and the Shulamite exchanging their vows of love for one another. The shepherd's love for the Shulamite has triumphed.

How suitable it is that this song should end by directing our thoughts to the coming of Christ, to our complete vindication at the judgment seat, and to the unending years of bliss that are to be ours with Him, our wonderful, adorable Lord.

Having seen the overall plan of this fascinating devotional poem, let us now go back to the beginning and explore each segment of the song for the lessons it has for us in the love-life of the soul.

I. AN HOUR OF TROUBLE

Song of Solomon 1:1-8

THE SONG OF SOLOMON is a book of romance. It begins with the Shulamite woman, a woman the philandering king greatly desired to marry. She has been overtaken by an unexpected disaster: she has been seen and snared by Solomon.

The Shulamite's home was at Shunem near Mount Gilboa, a place rich in Bible history, located at the southwest foot of Little Hermon, three miles north of Jezreel. The Shulamite lived with her widowed mother and several brothers—farmers and shepherds—who were jealous for their younger sister's reputation.

One day when entering a garden the young Shulamite found herself unexpectedly in the presence of King Solomon, who was visiting the area with certain members of his court. Struck by the beauty of this country girl the king gave orders for her to be taken to his pavilion. The court women there see the Shulamite and listen to her with astonishment. Instinctively, in her reaction against the compromising situation, the Shulamite turns her thoughts toward her true love, a local shepherd boy. She speaks of three things about him: the fervor the shepherd had shown toward her, the fragrance he had shed upon her, and the freedom he had shared with her.

A. THE FERVOR THE SHEPHERD HAD SHOWN TOWARD HER (1:2)

"Let him kiss me with the kisses of his mouth: for thy love is better than wine." She recalls that his love *was tenderly expressed.*

"Oh!" cried the Shulamite as her heart went out to her shepherd and she thought of his love, "Oh, for a kiss!" It is the heart cry of one who has tasted the love of the Lord Jesus and who longs for His love to be expressed in a tender, tangible way.

The Lord Jesus, when Judas came with that mob, said to him: "Betrayest thou the Son of man with a kiss?" A *kiss?* It need hardly be said that a kiss is an expression of love. It is this that made the treachery of Judas so obscene. He betrayed the Saviour with a kiss. That which normally expresses tenderness Judas used in treachery.

The love of the Shulamite's shepherd *was tremendously exciting.* "For thy love," she mused, "is better than wine." Wine is intoxicating: it inflames the blood, it goes to the head, it excites the whole being, it warms and fires the inner man. "Thy love is better than wine" because wine can be a mocker and lead to folly. But not so the love of Christ. It excites but it never degrades or defiles, never leaves us bereft of reason and responsibility. It is better than wine!

Perhaps we have become so accustomed to the great truths of the gospel that they rarely excite us anymore. Some of us have sung since we were children Anna B. Warner's beautiful hymn, "Jesus loves me, this I know, for the Bible tells me so." Think of the tremendous truth in those simple words! It is better than wine.

"Jesus loves me!" The Son of the living God, the Creator of all the suns and stars of space, the One whom angels worship, He who inhabits eternity has given His heart to us! Paul never ceased to marvel at it. "He loved me!" he exclaimed, "He loved *me* and gave Himself for *me!*" To think that He loves *me,* one not worthy to be called a Christian, one less than the least of all saints, one who deserves the title, "chief of sinners," He loved *me!* (cf. Galatians 2:20; 1 Timothy 1:15) Charles H. Gabriel has expressed it thus:

> I marvel that He would descend from His throne divine,
> To rescue a soul so rebellious and proud as mine;
> That He should extend His great love unto such as I,
> Sufficient to own, to redeem, and to justify!
> Oh, it is wonderful that He should care for me
>   Enough to die for me.
> Oh, it is wonderful, wonderful to me!
>
> CHARLES H. GABRIEL

The Shulamite recalls the fervor her beloved had shown toward her. The thought of it made her long for more. It is worth noting that the word translated "love" is plural in the original, "loves." One taste will never do. Who could be satisfied with one kiss from a beloved?[1]

B. THE FRAGRANCE THE SHEPHERD HAD SHED UPON HER (1:3-6)

The Shulamite continues to soliloquize about her absent

---

[1]John Nelson Darby, *The Holy Scriptures: A New Translation from the Original Languages* (Kingston-on-Thames: Stow Hill Bible and Tract Depot), 1950 ed. Darby reminds us that the word is the same one which gives us the name *David.*

but beloved shepherd. First *she talks about him* and then *she talks about herself.* These are the two most interesting persons in the world to one in love! Let there be a thousand people present, the lovers have eyes only for each other.

1. She Talks About Him (1:3-4)

The Shulamite reminds herself of *the magnificence of his presence:* "Because of the savor of thy good ointments thy name is as ointment poured forth." Darby translates it: "Thine ointments savour sweetly: Thy name is as an ointment poured forth."

A person wearing perfume coming into a room attracts immediate attention. The perfume announces the presence. Similarly, the very name of the beloved conjures up for the Shulamite a sense of his presence.

Let a young girl in love begin to doodle on a piece of paper and soon she will be writing down his name. It is a name she finds dear, it sets the joybells ringing in her heart. His name has for her "the savor of good ointment poured forth."

It is significant that God, for the most part and especially in the Old Testament, revealed Himself to men by means of His names. Elohim! Adonai! Jehovah! The Old Testament saints fell in love with those names, especially the name Jehovah; and in so doing they fell in love with Him of whom the names so eloquently spoke. They wrote them down under the guiding impulse of the Holy Spirit again and again, this way and that:

Jehovah-Jireh—The LORD who provides (Genesis 22:14)
Jehovah-Nissi—The LORD our banner—The LORD who protects (Exodus 17:15)

Jehovah-Shalom—The LORD who gives peace (Judges 6:24)
Jehovah-Tsidkenu—The LORD our righteousness—The LORD who pardons (Jeremiah 23:6; 33:16)
Jehovah-Shammah—The LORD who is there—The LORD who is present (Ezekiel 48:35)
Jehovah-Roi—The LORD my Shepherd—The LORD who pastors (Psalm 23:1)
Jehovah-Mekkadishkem—The LORD who sanctifies—The LORD who purifies (Exodus 31:13)
Jehovah-Ropheka—The LORD who heals—The LORD the physician (Exodus 15:26)
Jehovah-Sabbaoth—The LORD of hosts—The LORD of all power (1 Samuel 1:3)
Jehovah-Elyon—The LORD most high—The LORD who is preeminent (Psalm 7:17; 47:2)

To the Old Testament saints the name Jehovah was an ointment poured forth shedding its fragrance over all.

New Testament saints think of Him as JESUS. If ever there was a name that, "as ointment poured forth," shed a fragrance over all of human life it is the name of Jesus! It is the saving name: "Thou shalt call His name JESUS: for He shall save His people from their sins" (Matthew 1:21). It is the sanctifying name. We are to do all things, in word and deed, in the name of the Lord Jesus (cf. Colossians 3:17). It is the sovereign name. "At the name of Jesus every knee should bow" (Philippians 2:10). It is the name that "charms our fears and bids our sorrows cease." It is the name that, as "music in the sinner's ears, brings life and health and peace."

> There is no name so sweet on earth
> No name so sweet in Heaven,
> The name before His wondrous birth,
> To Christ the Saviour given.
> GEORGE W. BETHUNE

Jesus! Oh how sweet the name!
Jesus! Every day the same!
Jesus! Let all saints proclaim
Thy worthy praise for ever.
W. C. MARTIN

We sing about that name until we have filled half our hymnbook with its charms. It is the name that secures for us His presence, for He Himself promised: "Where two or three are gathered together in My name, there am I in the midst of them" (Matthew 18:20).

The Shulamite talks, too, about *the magnetism of his personality* (1:3b-4). First, he *could draw others:* "Thy name is as ointment poured forth, therefore do the virgins love thee" (1:3b). Mason Good, the hymnwriter, renders the verse like this:

Rich Thy perfumes, but richer far than they
The countless charms that round Thy person play;
Thy name alone, more fragrant than the rose
Thrills every maid, where'er its fragrance flows.
MASON GOOD

The Shulamite's beloved drew others to himself. And so does our Shepherd! To know Him is to want Him.

The Shulamite's beloved *could deliver her:* "Draw me, we will run after thee" (1:4a). Then she adds the reason for the sense of urgency: "The King hath brought me into his chambers" (1:4b). She feels herself in peril. But the shepherd can save her! She calls out to him.

How could a country lad, a shepherd boy, ever combat a king? How could he confront Solomon in all his pomp and power? How could he even get through to the inner compartments of the king's pavilion? We are not told. This is not the language of logic, this is the language of love. Love knows no obstacles, love "climbs every mountain, swims every sea"! Love always finds a way.

What a wonderful Lord we have. He can draw others, He can deliver us! There is no prison this world can devise which can keep a loving, trusting heart from Christ or keep Him from coming to those who call upon Him.

God would have us listen to the language of the heart. After all, we get into Heaven heartfirst, not headfirst! When it comes to the bottom line of belief, when we are faced with some crushing situation for which we have no solution, then is the time to trust all to love. When it comes to a showdown in the soul between seeming fact and simple faith, then is the time to trust the heart rather than the head.

Think of that great Pauline passage on love in 1 Corinthians 13: "Charity [love] . . . beareth all things, believeth all things, hopeth all things, endureth all things. Charity [love] never faileth." J. B. Phillips modernizes that magnificent passage: "Love knows no limit to its endurance, no end to its trust, no fading of its hope; it can outlast anything. Love never fails."[2] So trust your heart, especially when your heart is telling you to trust the Lord.

Every circumstance militated against the shepherd ever being able to deliver the Shulamite, but at the end of the story we discover that he *did* deliver her, though we are not told how. He did! Love found a way.

Her beloved *could delight all:* "We will be glad and rejoice in thee, we will remember thy love more than wine: the upright love thee" (1:4b,c,d).

---

[2]J. B. Phillips, *The New Testament in Modern English* (Student Edition) (New York: The Macmillan Co.), page 361.

The Shulamite strikes a threefold chord. The first note is one of *rejoicing*. What an anchor that is to the soul when things go wrong, when circumstances threaten and appall. The great antidote is to rejoice, not because of what has happened, but *in* our Beloved, because, after all, *He* has not changed and He still loves us.

The second note is one of *remembrance:* "We will remember thy love more than wine." That is the second secret of a victorious life—first rejoicing, then remembrance. The Lord Jesus instituted a feast of remembrance just before He went to the cross. He spread the emblems on the table and He told the disciples that henceforth, regularly, as a deliberate act of worship, they were to remember Him. To become preoccupied with our situation is to forget our Saviour. The Shulamite countered all the problems of life with the simple remembrance of her shepherd.

The third note is one of *righteousness:* "the upright love thee." The character of the shepherd was such that upright people loved him. Solomon had no love for this shepherd, neither did the women of his court. To love him called for a state of soul which was entirely lacking in them.

That is why so many people fail to see beauty in the Lord Jesus. It is not that they lack the intelligence or the emotional capacity. Failure to love the Lord is a moral, not a mental problem. It is the upright, that is, the righteous, who love Him. One cannot love Solomon *and* the shepherd—they represent different worlds, different philosophies, different standards, different ways of life. A person cannot love this present evil world and Christ.

These three things—rejoicing, remembrance, and righteousness—are the best protection we have against this world in which we live, a world so determined to draw us away.

2. She Talks About Herself (1:5-6)

The court women are still there and suddenly the Shulamite seems to see them—their silken gowns, their jewels, the latest fashions. She looks at herself in her home-spun clothes with her sun-tanned arms and suddenly she is aware of the contrast.

First *she describes herself:* "I am black, but comely, O ye daughters of Jerusalem, as the tents of Kedar, as the curtains of Solomon," or, "I am dark like the tents of Kedar but I am as beautiful as the curtains of Solomon" (1:5).

The name Kedar is generally applied to the nomadic Ishmaelites and in Scripture is frequently a descriptive term for Arabic Bedouin tribes in general. The tents of the Bedouins were usually made of black goatskins. The Shulamite, comparing herself with the women of Solomon's harem, was momentarily embarrassed by her dark hue: "I am like the tents of Kedar."

She was tanned, surely, but it was most becoming. Although she might be dusky that did not detract from her natural beauty: "I am as beautiful as the curtains of Solomon," she exclaims, doubtless noting the gorgeous draperies of the royal tent.

It is good to accept ourselves for what we are. God sees beauty in each one of us and has a wise and wonderful purpose in making us the way we are. The Shulamite's natural beauty, tanned as it was by the sun, was far lovelier than the artificiality of the court women.

Consider the words of the Lord Jesus when, walking one day along a country road, He paused to pick up a wayside weed: "I say unto you, that even Solomon in all his glory was not arrayed like one of these" (Matthew 6:29). The glory of Solomon was on the outside; the glory of the lily grew from within. It was the same with the Shulamite. And so it should be with us.

I was staying in a home recently where a picture of a retarded child was pinned on the door of the refrigerator. The child was depicted as saying: "I know I'm *somebody* 'cause *God* don't make no junk." "I am black, but comely, O ye daughters of Jerusalem."

The Shulamite then *defends herself* (1:6a,b). She did not have to do that—it spoils the picture. It is a natural reaction, just the same. She says that *her background has been harsh* ("the sun hath looked upon me") and that *her brothers have been hostile* ("my mother's children were angry with me; they made me the keeper of the vineyards").

Her brothers had no sympathy with the Shulamite's love for her beloved. They had done all they could to separate them, taking her from the fields, where she had opportunities to meet him, and putting her in the vineyard to toil. They made it difficult for her to have those delightful times of communion with her love.

Often a believer's stiffest opposition comes from members of his own family. A new Christian may discover that his confession of faith in Christ stirs up a hornet's nest at home.

Some years ago we had a neighbor who would often talk about the Bible and seemed hungry for spiritual things, but rarely if ever attended church. Eventually she accepted the Lord Jesus as her Saviour. She came running over to my wife, her face beaming with joy, and exclaiming: "I see it! It's not by works! It's by faith!" She began to come to the church we attended and brought her little girl to Sunday school. The rest of her family exploded. One of them said: "If you don't stop going to that church I shall never speak to you again or visit your home." Her family ties were strong and the threat worked. She never did come back to our church nor did she ever again seek the company of my wife. Jesus said: "A man's foes shall be they of his own household" (Matthew 10:36).

The Shulamite described and defended herself, then went a step further—*she despises herself:* "But mine own vineyard have I not kept" (1:6c). She implies that she has been far too busy to spend hours combing her hair and painting her face like the court women. She has far too healthy an attitude for much introspection. Wisely she turns her thoughts back to her beloved.

C. THE FREEDOM THE SHEPHERD HAD SHARED WITH HER (1:7-8)

Her thoughts go back to days when she roamed the verdant pastures, able to meet with her shepherd and exchange mutual vows of love.

1. How That Freedom Is Recalled (1:7)

Longing for a fresh experience of that freedom she cries out: "Tell me, O thou whom my soul loveth, where thou feedest [thy flock], where thou makest they flock to rest at noon: for why should I be as one that turneth aside by the flocks of thy companions?" The last part of this verse is difficult. Rotherham puts it: "For why should I be as one that wrappeth a veil about her by the flocks of thy companions?" Darby is similar: "For why should I be as one veiled [or, roving] beside the flocks of thy companions?" Why indeed? That would not be liberty but license.

The Shulamite, in her perfumed prison, longs for the open air, the freedom of the fields. She does not desire freedom for freedom's sake, but for liberty to be with her beloved. She did not want to have to wander from flock to flock, veiling herself before her beloved's companions, in her search for him. She wanted the freedom that needed no veil.

The Lord's first mission on earth was designed to restore us to perfect freedom: "If the Son therefore shall make you free, ye shall be free indeed" (John 8:36). Satan would bring us into bondage to sin, to self, to situations. That is what Solomon tried to do to the Shulamite, but she had tasted real freedom and it made her impatient with Solomon's advances.

2. How That Freedom Is Ridiculed (1:8)

The Shulamite had cried out for the freedom she knew could be found with her beloved. The court women mocked her: "If thou know not, O thou fairest among women, go thy way forth by the footsteps of the flock, and feed thy kids beside the shepherds' tents." "Get thee forth in the footsteps of the flock, and pasture thy kids by the huts of the shepherds" (Rotherham).

Their words are full of sarcasm. "Don't you understand your position? Don't you realize what Solomon is offering you? If you don't appreciate it you had best get back to your backwoods life." That, of course, is exactly what she wished she could do. They despised what she prized.

II. AN HOUR OF TEMPTATION

Song of Solomon 1:9-11

THE SHULAMITE has been captured by Solomon and is virtually his prisoner. So far she has strengthened herself by keeping the thought of her beloved shepherd foremost in her mind.

What happens when Solomon with all his personal and positional magnificence, makes his first outright attempt to seduce the Shulamite away from her Shepherd? Here Solomon is not a type of Christ but a type of the tempter, and his offers are reminiscent of the offers of the world.

Temptation is real. Satan comes sometimes as an angel of light, as a roaring lion, as a serpent in the way. Sometimes he seeks to dazzle, to destroy, to deceive. The chief instrument he employs is the world—"the lust of the flesh, and the lust of the eyes, and the pride of life" (1 John 2:16). He tries flattery, filth, falsehood. His supreme objective is to get between the soul and Christ.

The historical story can be applied in two ways. We can apply it to the Church, and examine the ways in which Satan uses the world to draw away the Church, the betrothed of Christ, from her loyalty to the Lord. Or we can apply the incident to the Christian and see how Satan uses the world, of which he is both god and prince, to seduce the individual believer away from his commitment to Christ. Either way the story is rich in teaching.

A. SOLOMON'S PRAISE (1:9-10)

Solomon begins with a word of praise, with flattery. "I have compared thee, O my love, to a company of horses in Pharaoh's chariots. Thy cheeks are comely with rows of jewels, thy neck with chains of gold."

1. He Praises the Shulamite's Power (1:9)

She is like a company of horses in Pharaoh's chariots! "To a mare of mine in the chariots of Pharaoh have I likened thee my fair one" (Rotherham).

Solomon evidently thought that to be a flattering comparison. A horse in Pharaoh's chariots would no doubt impress him. It represented power. But it is doubtful whether the Shulamite would have been much impressed for the horse was an unclean animal in Israel. And what woman wants to be compared to a horse! "I have compared thee O my love to a company of horses in Pharaoh's chariots." It was a candid admission that the Shulamite was armed with the most formidable weapons, chastity and purity.

The Church is similarly armed. Well might the prince of darkness liken the Church to a company of horses in Pharaoh's chariots for the Church is panoplied in power! Men see her divided, torn asunder, split by factions, divisions, and quarrels. But the Church is armed with spiritual weapons which are mighty through God to the pulling down of strongholds. She is invincible, the gates of hell cannot prevail against her.

Solomon's mention of the Shulamite's power was a clever move. It is only as we are weak that we are truly strong. The Lord said to the Apostle Paul when, after desperate prayer, Paul besought the Lord to remove that "thorn in the flesh" that troubled him. "My grace is sufficient for thee: for My strength is made perfect in weakness" (2 Corinthians 12:9). The moment we begin to think we are strong then we are most vulnerable.

2. He Praises the Shulamite's Person (1:10)

"Thy cheeks are comely with rows of jewels, thy neck with chains of gold." The headdress of an oriental woman is often adorned with dangling beads or small ornaments such as coins. Solomon is praising not so much the natural beauty of the Shulamite as the trinkets he has set upon her. He thinks he has greatly improved upon her natural loveliness.

The world cannot appreciate the unadorned beauty of the Church. Take a worldling to a simple prayer meeting where some believers are gathered at the throne of grace and he will find nothing attractive. Take him to a gathering where the saints are sitting around an unadorned table contemplating a loaf of bread and a container of wine, lifting up their hearts in spiritual worship, and he will wonder at the plainness of it all. The world will at once want to improve and embellish. It will suggest a better meeting place, a more elaborate ritual, some gorgeous vestments, or orchestrated music. The early Church, in the days of its pristine power, managed with none of these things.

"Thy cheeks are comely with rows of jewels, thy neck with chains of gold." The great function of the neck, of course, is to uphold the head. Solomon has nothing to say about that. His desire is to put chains upon that neck, chains of gold perhaps, but chains just the same.

The Church's great purpose is to uphold the Head, Jesus

Christ. We are to set Him forth in all His glory before the world. Paul, in First Corinthians, in Romans, and in Ephesians, reminds us that the Church is the mystical body of Christ and that He is the Head of that body. The function of the neck is to exalt the head.

Satan cannot attack the risen, ascended Head of the Church. Nor can he sever the body from the Head; the union between Christ and His Church, while mystical, is not mythical, but has been forged by the living God Himself. Nothing can separate us from Christ (cf. Romans 8:39).

The true Church does not need the world's embellishments. Its treasure is in Heaven, its resources are in Christ. We do not despise beautiful or useful things, but the Church does not need "things" in order to function and grow.

The measure in which the Church depends on material things is the measure in which she is vulnerable, for when hostile forces come to power and turn against the Church they can soon rob it of its buildings and its wealth. The early Church conquered the Roman world from the catacombs. St. Basil's, in Moscow, today is a museum, not a place of worship. Years of unceasing persecution, however, have not enabled the communists to seduce the real Church. It is stronger, more dynamic, purer, more effective, and a greater power for God in Russia than it has ever been.[1]

---

[1]In 1979 I shared a conference at the New Brunswick Bible Institute, Victoria, Canada, with Elwyn Davies, an evangelist to the Slavic peoples. He had just returned from a prolonged visit to the Soviet Union. He had a thrilling story to tell of a Church living in revival in the face of constant persecution. Meetings would be jammed to capacity, with people standing in every available corner. Services would last for at least two hours with lengthy "after-services" often following the regular meetings. He found people hungry for the Word of God, witnessing boldly, and unintimidated by repression.

B. SOLOMON'S PROMISE (1:11)

"We will make thee borders of gold with studs of silver."
Foolish is the church that takes the world at its word! That
is what the church at Laodicea did. "I am rich, and increased with goods, and have need of nothing" was her
boast. "Thou art wretched, and miserable, and poor, and
blind, and naked," replied the Lord (Revelation 3:17).

Solomon now offers the Shulamite a crown of silver and
gold. Gold, in the Bible is linked with sovereignty and
silver with salvation. We must look closely at this offer of
Solomon for it symbolizes what the prince of this world
offers to the Church. We can be sure that an offer from
such a source is not what it seems to be.

1. Gold, the Symbol of Sovereignty (1:11a)

"We will make thee borders of gold." Gold was one of
the gifts the wise men brought from the east when they
came to Jerusalem inquiring for one "born king of the
Jews." It is a gift for a king, a queen. We need to beware,
however, when gold is offered as bait. Solomon believed
that every woman has her price. The world's attitude
toward the Church is much the same.

There are two things we instinctively associate with a
crown of gold—*rule* and *riches.*

What was it Satan offered to the Lord Jesus in the temptation? Royal power! He took Him up into a high mountain and spread before Him all the kingdoms of the world:
"You see these kingdoms? You can have them—the kingdoms, the power, the glory! It can all be yours just so long
as you worship me" (Luke 4:6-7). The evil one, in offering
all that power to Christ, did not offer Him *dunamis,* real,

absolute power. He offered Him *exousia,* power subject to
another power, delegated authority. The real power he
proposed to keep for himself. Jesus refused the offer.

Exousia is what Satan repeatedly offers the Church. All
too often the professing church has been willing to accept
the very thing the Saviour refused. The outward, professing, worldly church has increased its position and pomp,
but it has no real power. It has temporal power (though
it is power that waxes and wanes), and for that it has traded
away its spiritual power.

Solomon knew the real power of the Shulamite and
respected it. Later on in the book he will mention it again
and again. By offering her a crown of gold, at a price, he
was hoping she would give up that real power, which
derived its strength from her fidelity to her shepherd, by
yielding herself to another.

"We will make thee borders of gold." This promise
hinted at the resources which were Solomon's to command. From his standpoint of wealth and power, he might
well have thought that the affections of a poor country girl
could be bought. How little he knew her!

2. Silver, the Symbol of Salvation (1:11b)

In the Bible, silver is frequently used as a symbol of
salvation. Two people were sold for silver, Joseph and
Jesus, relating silver to the price of life.

By reason of its purity, its resistance to corrosion, and
its ability to withstand the fiercest heat, silver is a beautiful
picture of that lovely life of the Lord Jesus which was
yielded up on the cross of Calvary as a redemption price
for sin.

In Israel, when the tribes were numbered for service or

for war, it was mandatory for each individual counted to bring with him to the priest a ransom for his soul of half a shekel of silver, "after the shekel of the sanctuary" (Exodus 30:11-16). Each man, no matter whether he were rich or poor was required to bring the same amount. Each person, weighed in the balances of God was lost, needing to be redeemed, and the just and perfect standard of God in the sanctuary saw to it that a perfect ransom was paid. The priest would not accept one iota more or less. The great point of all this is that God builds on the basis of redemption and on that basis alone.

"We will make thee studs of silver," said Solomon to the Shulamite. Solomon knew all about the atonement money, the silver which was the basis for atonement in the symbolic language of the tabernacle. He borrows from the type and offers silver to the young shepherd girl. It would be worthless silver, accepted at the price of the denial of her beloved. Solomon's use of silver debased the whole concept which lay behind the sanctification by God of that precious metal as a symbol of redemption.

We well might beware of any "salvation" which comes to us by way of the great tempter of mankind. Just as gold offered to the Shulamite by Solomon symbolized an offer of pomp, not power, so the silver symbolized an offer of religion, not redemption. It is not in Satan's power to offer men salvation. He therefore offers a counterfeit salvation based on good works, human merit, and self effort. True salvation is through the precious blood of Christ and that Satan both hates and fears.

"We will make thee borders of gold with studs of silver." The Shulamite turned coldly away from the promises of her tempter. What Solomon had to offer was trash compared to her beloved. She would rather have her shepherd. We would rather have our Shepherd, too.

III. AN HOUR OF TENDERNESS

Song of Solomon 1:12—2:7

As THIS SECTION of the song begins, the shepherd comes to the Shulamite. He makes no attempt to get her away from her restraining circumstances. He simply does what he can to strengthen and encourage her and to assure her that he loves her and is watching over her. How that enterprising shepherd was able to be alone with his dear one in that perfumed prison we do not know. It is sufficient that he came and that the song now celebrates the hour of tenderness.

Is not that the way with us? When our hearts are over-whelmed with the things which have overtaken us, our lovely Lord draws near in special ways to strengthen and sustain us through it all.

A. LOVE'S BRAVERY (1:12-14)

It is sometimes difficult in the Song of Solomon to decide just who is speaking and to whom. A clue is found in the gender of the pronouns and it is clear that the Shulamite is the one who is talking here.

1. The Shulamite Explains Her Loyalty (1:12)

"While the king sitteth at his table, my spikenard sendeth forth the smell thereof." Spikenard was an aromatic oil extracted from a plant which grew in eastern India. It was a rare and costly perfume. Mary of Bethany gave spikenard as her love gift to the Lord Jesus Christ shortly before he went to Calvary. When she broke the alabaster container which held the precious unguent the whole house was instantly filled with its fragrance (cf. Matthew 26:7).

The Shulamite calls her beloved "my spikenard." Her soul was alive with the lingering fragrance of his love. She could not forget him even if she wished. Have we told the Lord lately that He is a sweet fragrance to our souls?

2. The Shulamite Expresses Her Love (1:13-14)

The Shulamite, gives expression to her love; *she rejoices in her prospect:* "A bundle of myrrh is my well-beloved unto me; he [or "it," the bundle of myrrh] shall lie all night betwixt my breasts" (1:13).

Like spikenard, myrrh was a fragrant perfume. It was extracted from an Arabian balsam and was widely used both at weddings and funerals in Palestine. In Israel's religious rituals myrrh was used as one of the important ingredients of the holy anointing oil.

The myrrh reminded the Shulamite of her beloved. She even slept with it close to her heart in prospect of a coming wedding day and of the closest intimacy.

Then *she rejoices in his person:* "My beloved is unto me as a cluster of camphire in the vineyards of En-gedi" (1:14). Most translators render the word camphire as henna or cypress flowers, clusters of cream-colored flowers which grow abundantly in the Holy Land. En-gedi, sometimes called "the city of palm trees," was located thirty miles southeast of Jerusalem on the west shore of the Dead Sea. It was a wild, desolate region, full of rocks and caves but saved from barrenness by the spring which bubbled up out of the mountainside about six hundred feet above sea level, providing water for the vineyards. The henna flowers of En-gedi symbolize beauty where one would expect barrenness. The Shulamite's shepherd was the flower of the vineyard to her soul.

What a wonderful lesson there is in all this for our own souls. Let us, like the Shulamite, rejoice in our prospect! Let us hug to our hearts, like a bundle of myrrh, the treasured truths we have of the cross and the coming of our Lord, which point us back to His burial and forward to the bridal feast when we shall hold Him to our hearts, rejoicing in His person.

> I'd rather have Jesus than silver or gold,
>   I'd rather be His than have riches untold,
> I'd rather have Jesus than houses or land,
>   I'd rather be led by His nail-pierced hand;
> Than to be the king of a vast domain
>   And to be held in sin's dread sway;
> I'd rather have Jesus than anything
>   This world affords today.
>   GEORGE BEVERLY SHEA

B. LOVE'S BEAUTY (1:15—2:2)

1. The Shepherd Thinks of the Shulamite and of Peace (1:15)

"Behold, thou art fair, my love; behold, thou art fair;

thou hast doves' eyes." She reminds him of a dove, a
symbol of peace. It was a dove which brought the olive
twig back to Noah, an evident token that God's wrath had
been assuaged and that all was at peace on the planet. The
dove, the one bird used for sacrifice, was a clean bird
according to Jewish law. It is the only bird that makes
itself the voluntary prisoner of man. It has snowy white
plumage, round eyes, and a strong homing instinct. Frequently the dove is used in Scripture as a symbol of the
Holy Spirit.

As the shepherd looked upon his beloved he saw a
gentle, home-loving, sacrificial person who displayed the
characteristics we associate with the Holy Spirit.

This, surely, is what the Lord Jesus desires to see in
us— the reflected glories and graces of His Holy Spirit. Are
our eyes round with wonder as we gaze upon Him?

2. The Shulamite Thinks of the Shepherd and of Paradise (1:16—2:1)

The prospect she covets: "Behold, thou art fair, my beloved,
yea pleasant: yea our couch is green [verdant, covered with
leaves]" (1:16). She looks forward to the day when they will
be married and she pictures some secret forest glade as the
place of their honeymoon.

The place she conceives: "The beams of our house are cedar
and our rafters of fir" (1:17). "The beams of our house are
cedars, and our rafters are cypresses" (Darby). She sees a
primeval paradise or the fair garden of Eden, a place of
simplicity and sanctity, glorious beyond words because
they are together there.

The problem she considers: "I am the rose of Sharon, and
the lily of the valleys" (2:1). She could see herself only as

a meadow saffron flower. How could he, her wonderful shepherd, see anything at all in her?

Every believer contemplates the same problem from time to time. "I am just a wayside weed and He the lofty cedar! How could He ever care for me? There are so many in the world nobler, purer, greater, better. Why me?"

3. The Shepherd Thinks of the Shulamite and of Purity (2:2)

The Shulamite's heart is swiftly set at rest for once more the beloved speaks: "As the lily among thorns, so is my love among the daughters." The Palestinian lily was a flower which normally grew in the midst of wheat. The women of Solomon's court, for all their expensive clothes, overpowering perfumes, and costly jewels were thorns; but the Shulamite was as lovely and as royal as the lily with its rich, dark, purple petals.

That, too, is how the Lord sees us despite all our faults and failings—as lilies in the midst of a wilderness of thorns.

The Lord Jesus once picked a wayside weed, one of these meadow lilies. "I say unto you," He said to His disciples, "that Solomon in all his glory was not arrayed like one of these" (Matthew 6:29). The glory of Solomon was mostly external and artificial; the glory of the lily was part of the intrinsic nature of the plant itself. As His eye rests upon us He sees us arrayed in His beauty and clothed in the regal splendor of His finished work of grace.

C. Love's Bounty (2:3-6)

The mark of love is that it finds its chief delight in giving. Like the Shulamite we think of our Beloved and how He has expressed His love for us in giving. "Christ loved the Church," says Paul, "and gave Himself for it." Then, making it even more personal he adds: "He loved me and gave Himself for me."

The Shulamite describes her beloved's bounty in two ways. She thinks first of *the bounty of a forest:* "As the apple tree among the trees of the wood, so is my beloved among the sons. I sat down under his shadow with great delight, and his fruit was sweet to my taste" (2:3). She is grateful for *its protection:* "I sat down under his shadow with great delight." As on a hot, humid day a leafy tree will provide welcome protection from the burning sun, so the Shulamite found her protection in her beloved. Just to sit in the conscious knowledge of his presence, his nearness, his strength, his protection, was heaven to her soul.

Surely, we do not often enough just simply enjoy the Lord! He is there to protect us from the burden and heat of the day, when the way becomes wearisome and we feel crushed by the circumstances of life. This is a time when we should deliberately stop to enjoy Him.

The Shulamite is grateful also for the tree's *provision:* "I sat down under his shadow with great delight, and his fruit was sweet to my taste." She described it as the *bounty of a feast:* "He brought me to the banqueting house" (2:4a). At that moment Solomon was off regaling himself at his table. The shepherd could not provide such a *banquet,* but what he could set before the Shulamite would have been seasoned with love, and that would turn any morsel into a feast.

One of these days we are going to sup with our Beloved in the glory land and, when that day dawns, He will set before us a banquet the like of which this world has never seen. Right now, He spreads a table for us in the wilderness (Psalm 78:19). It is not a table loaded with the things that the children of this world would desire for only two items appear on it.

> Only bread and only wine,
> Yet to faith the solemn sign,
> Of the heavenly and divine—
> We give Thee thanks, O Lord.
>   HORATIUS BONAR

Our hearts are full because *He* has spread a table for *us!* The highest archangels of glory know nothing of the privilege which is ours to gather in His name, to know Him present in our midst, to sit down in His presence, and to address ourselves to the bread and wine upon the table, those rich emblems of His body broken and His blood poured forth.

The banner: "He brought me into his banqueting house and his banner over me was love" (2:4b). Flapping over Solomon's pavilion, perhaps, were the ensigns of all the tribes over which he ruled, the banners making a notable showing against the blue of the sky.

The Shulamite had a banner which meant more to her than all the banners of Solomon. Beneath that banner she found all that her heart desired.

The beloved: It was the thought of her beloved that made everything else worthwhile. The Shulamite tells how his love overwhelms her: "Stay me with flagons, comfort me with apples: for I am sick of love" (2:5). She is absolutely overwhelmed at the thought of the love of her beloved and his love overjoys her: "His left hand is under my head, and his right hand doth embrace me" (2:6). Her beloved is holding her to himself. She is wholly his and he is altogether hers. Love is a very intimate thing.

D. LOVE'S BOUNDARY (2:7)

Love does not trespass where law forbids. It is lust that does that, not love. Love knows where to draw the line, where to recognize the boundaries between right and wrong. Lust blunders on into sin, but love observes God's laws. Love knows how to wait and how to keep itself pure, observing love's boundary.

The last verse of the section gives us a study in contrasts. First we have *the masculinity of the worldly women of the court.* The Shulamite says to them, "I charge you, O ye daughters of Jerusalem." Scholars say that the word "you" and the accompanying verbs are masculine, yet the subject is clearly feminine. As it is not common to find this grammatical construction in the text, it suggests that true femininity has been lost. The painted beauties of Solomon's court knew nothing of restraint, modesty, or decency.

We then have *the modesty of the shy Shulamite from the country:* "I charge you, O ye daughters of Jerusalem, by the roes and by the hinds of the field, that ye stir not up, nor awake my love, till he please." The Hebrew word awake means to incite. The Shulamite is saying that her passions are not to be excited, awakened, stirred up. Darby comments: "nor awaken love till it please."

It would seem that the Shulamite's beloved has left her and the court women have come back with the deliberate intent of trying to arouse the young girl's passions so that Solomon will find her an easy mark. However, the Shulamite had clearly drawn love's boundaries in her life and she refused to have anything to do with that which would stimulate passion and desire. Her love was reserved for her shepherd and that love was clean and pure.

It is a lesson that very much needs to be underlined today. We are living in an age when passion is for sale. The great tempter knows how to arouse passion. We need to draw the line with a firm, deliberate hand by refusing to consider for a single moment things which would illicitly awaken desire.

IV. AN HOUR OF TRUTH

Song of Solomon 2:8 — 3:5

A. THE LOVE OF THE SHEPHERD (2:8-14)

1. The Coming of the Shepherd (2:8-9)

The Shulamite describes him: "The voice of my beloved! behold, he cometh leaping upon the mountains, skipping upon the hills" (2:8). *His voice* brought all the music of Heaven into her heart. It was the first thing that arrested her attention. She could pick that voice out of a thousand, it was her beloved's.

Surely the first thing our Beloved would have us remember is His voice. It was this voice that Adam heard while walking in the garden in the cool of the day; that cast the demons out of Mary's tortured soul; that stilled the tempest of that Galilean sea; that the bacillus of leprosy heard and fled. It is the voice that:

> . . .calls us o'er the tumult
>   Of our life's wild restless sea!
> Day by day that sweet voice soundeth,
>   Saying, "Christian, follow Me!"
>   MRS. CECIL F. ALEXANDER

When the Lord Jesus would draw someone to Himself He speaks through His inspired Word.

The Shulamite remembered the shepherd's *vigor:* "Behold he cometh, leaping upon the mountains, skipping upon the hills." The word *he* is emphatic and could be rendered "this very one." What a picture of health, boundless energy, and joy! He is coming to be with her and nothing can hold him back!

That is what our Beloved thinks of us! John the Baptist said of the coming of the Lord Jesus that the crooked places would be made straight before Him, the rough places would be made smooth, the mountains would be leveled, and the valleys would be filled (Luke 3:5). Place a hundred obstacles before Him and He will overcome them all!

The Lord Jesus laid aside His glory, the glory that He had with the Father before the worlds began, and stooped to be born into the human family by way of the virgin's womb. He entered His ministry in the face of ridicule, opposition, and unbelief to face Gethsemane, Gabbatha, Golgotha, and the grave. He was spat upon, beaten, scourged, crowned with thorns, and nailed to a cross. He died beneath the wrath and curse of God. He laid in death for three days and three nights while the entire universe held its breath. But He came bursting forth from the tomb! We ask ourselves why He should come thus, in all the enormous energy of His deity, to pay such a price for us. There is only one answer: He loves us!

> Love found a way to redeem my soul,
> Love found a way that could make me whole;
> Love sent my Lord to the cross of shame,
> Love found a way! O praise His holy name!
>   CONSTANCE B. REID

Note how *the Shulamite discerns him:* "My beloved is like a roe or a young hart: behold, he standeth behind our wall, he looketh forth at the windows, showing himself through the lattice" (2:9).

True love never forces itself. The shepherd, with true sensitivity, as timid as a wild creature of the woods, peers around the wall and glances in at the window. He does not trespass where he is not invited. Walls and windows suggest man-made obstacles. These are natural obstacles erected between the soul and the Saviour, but there are also obstacles which we put up ourselves. The Lord Jesus will never force Himself upon us. So careful is He not to override our will, He simply reveals Himself to us, and leaves the next move up to us.

The Shulamite recalls how slow she was to respond on the occasion she describes. Her lack of willingness resulted in the quiet withdrawal of the shepherd.

2. The Call of the Shepherd (2:10-14)

Before he went away the shepherd called to the Shulamite with a threefold message appealing to his beloved's will, mind, and heart. His call beautifully sums up for us the call of the Lord Jesus to the human heart.

The shepherd's call was *volitional (to the will) to recognize a new lord:* "My beloved spake, and said unto me, Rise up, my love, my fair one, and come away" (2:10).

The sovereignty of God surely takes into account other wills, brought into existence by the will of God. To each of us is given a measure of volition and power of choice within certain bounds, decreed by Himself and set to a large extent by our mortality, frailty, and humanity. There can be no question that, in the end, God works out all things in conformity to His own perfect will. Nevertheless, within the limits He has set for us, we do have the power to choose.

Statements such as: "Whosoever will may come" and "wilt thou be made whole?" and "choose you this day whom you will serve" mean we have some measure of sovereignty ourselves, and are moral agents. The Lord Jesus frequently addresses Himself to our wills. The first call of the shepherd was to the will. "Rise up my love, my fair one, and come away." It was a call to be united with the shepherd, to leave the old way of life, to have a new lord. That is where the gospel makes its volitional contact with the soul.

The shepherd's call was also *logical (to the mind) to receive a new life* (2:11-13). What a wonderful life he sets before the Shulamite, embracing all the dimensions of time—*past, present,* and *future.* "For, lo, the winter is past, the rain is over and gone" (2:11). The storms of life are ended, a new season is about to begin, summer suns are on the way.

The Lord Jesus has dealt with the *past.* He died for all our sins, taking our enormous indebtedness upon Himself and paying it in full. Those cold, wintry experiences of life which we always had to face alone, we now can face with Him! From henceforth there will always be a ray of light even in the darkest sky. Moreover we can look forward to eternal sunshine in a land of fadeless day, beyond the reach of wind and storm.

The shepherd's call is also to new life that relates to the *present:* "The flowers appear on the earth; the time of the singing of birds is come, and the voice of the turtle [dove] is heard in our land" (2:12). It is to be a life of *beauty,* the vigorous, prolific, exciting life of spring which carpets the fields with flowers and fills the air with fragrance.

Our beloved Shepherd wishes to fill our lives with *beauty* instead of the bleakness and barrenness of life's cold, stormy winter. He desires to introduce into our lives all the beauties which glorified His life on earth—love, joy, peace, all the fruits of the Spirit.

It is to be a life of *bliss:* "The time of the spring-song hath come" (Rotherham). Instead of sorrow and sadness He wishes to bring sweetness and song. "I am come," He said, "that they might have life, and that they might have it more abundantly" (John 10:10).

It is to be a life of *blessing.* The turtle dove is a beautiful symbol of that wondrous Holy Spirit of God who is pure, gentle, and willing to make His home with man, the one who brings into a human heart all the blessings of God in Christ. What a blessing it is for a land to hear His voice.

The shepherd's call embraced the *future* as well. It took into consideration the Shulamite's present restrictive circumstances and was filled with rich promise for the future: "The fig tree putteth forth her green figs, and the vines with the tender grape give a good smell. Arise, my love, my fair one, and come away" (2:13).

The Lord Jesus took up the symbolism of the vine and transferred it to Himself and thence to those who would be mystically united with Him (John 15). The tender grapes, so lacking in the nation of Israel, would be found in the lives of those who dealt "in the vine," that is, in Himself. The vine is thus associated with the beginning of the church age.

The fig tree is associated with the end of the church age. Shortly before going to Calvary, Jesus deliberately cursed a fig tree because of its deceptiveness. Deprived of His blessing, the fig tree swiftly withered, much to the astonishment of the disciples (cf. Matthew 21:19). It was the only judgment miracle Jesus ever performed and depicted the drying up of the Jewish nation. In His Olivet discourse, shortly afterwards, He announced that the fig tree would revive at the end of the age. That is, Jewish national life would once again flourish on the earth. Moreover, the rebirth of Israel, in the last days, would herald the end times, the end of the church age, and the coming again of Christ to reign.

"The fig tree putteth forth her green figs. . . . Arise, my love, my fair one, and come away." From the standpoint of the shepherd, the prospect was glorious. All nature proclaimed new life! The Shulamite should be ready for instant departure.

The whole passage is full of rich meaning for us today. The Church, the glorious bride of Christ, is about to be delivered from its present restrictive surroundings. The Shepherd is coming to snatch us away. The signs of new life are everywhere to be seen. Most significant of all, Israel has been revived and is back in the land enjoying a dynamic national life. We should be ready for instant departure. Our Shepherd has planned for us life in a new dimension, life filled with *beauty, bliss,* and *blessing* far beyond anything ever experienced in this present scene.

The shepherd's call to the Shulamite was also *emotional (to the heart) to realize a new love:* "O my dove, that art in the clefts of the rock, in the secret places of the stairs [the hiding places of the cliff], let me see thy countenance, let me hear thy voice; for sweet is thy voice, and thy countenance is comely" (2:14). The shepherd longs for a response from the one to whom he has given his heart. Love, by its very nature, is willing to give and give, but to reach its highest bliss, love must be returned.

Thus our own wonderful Shepherd comes to us with an appeal to the heart. He pleads for a response from us. He longs to hear our voice. Already He sees in us the characteristics of the dove, the fruits of the Spirit. Already He sees us in Himself, the place of security, the cleft of the Rock. His heart longs for some willing response from us. Why do we keep Him waiting so long?

> Jesus calls us! By Thy mercy,
>   Saviour, may we hear the call;
> Give our hearts to Thy obedience,
>   Serve and love Thee best of all!
>   MRS. C. F. ALEXANDER

B. THE LOVE OF THE SHULAMITE (2:15—3:5)

The Shulamite tells the court women about her love for the shepherd.

Even a casual reading of the story reveals the simple fact that the shepherd's love for her is greater and more vigorous than her love for him. He will allow no obstacles to come between them. However, while she loves him and remains loyal to him, at times she does allow hindrances to come between them.

There is no comparison between the love of the Lord Jesus for us and our own feeble love for Him. Indeed, as John says, "We love Him, because He first loved us" (1 John 4:19). He never wavers in His boundless affection, never allows anything to come between us. Yet our love for Him is weak, spasmodic, so easily turned aside. It is strong enough, perhaps, to turn away wickedness and even worldliness, but how often it is overwhelmed by the cares and concerns of life.

1. A Hindered Love (2:15-17)

The Shulamite's love was hindered by a protective family, by a prohibitive society, as represented by the watchmen, and by a permissive atmosphere. The company in which she found herself was not conducive to keeping alive a vital, vibrant love for her absent shepherd. On the contrary, it was deliberately set to involve her in a compromising alliance with the world as represented by Solomon. It sapped away at her resolve to be true to her shepherd.

The Shulamite's problem (2:15): The Shulamite reminisces about the hostility toward her beloved which she had been forced to face at home. When her brothers discovered that their sister had given her heart to the shepherd and was secretly meeting with him, they took her away from the flock and placed her in the vineyard instead. "Take us the foxes, the little foxes, that spoil the vines: for our vines have tender grapes." Their objective was simple. Doubtless, they had the best of intentions—to preserve their sister's honor—and hoped that by isolating her from her shepherd they would succeed in making her forget him.

When a person comes to Christ the family may, out of ignorance of spiritual things, endeavor to intervene. "A man's foes," said the Lord Jesus, "shall be they of his own household" (Matthew 10:36).

Sometimes the opposition is violent, sometimes subtle. With the Shulamite, the family simply took her out of circulation. Her work in the vineyard, however, seems to have been the very thing which led to her capture by Solomon (6:11). But her brothers do not seem to have been upset about that! In some cases the unsaved members of a new believer's family would rather see their loved one become involved in something worldly than openly profess love for Christ.

The Shulamite recounts to the court women her past problem. The immediate problem she was facing was not that dissimilar. She had already been hindered from being with the shepherd.

The Shulamite's Passion (2:16-17): Persecution often backfires. Instead of intimidating the new believer it often has the opposite effect. Far from being discouraged by the attitude of her family, the Shulamite had given herself more fully and freely to her beloved in passionate *loyalty:* "My beloved is mine, and I am his: he feedeth among the lilies. Until the day break, and the shadows flee away" (2:16-17a).

Nobody can come between our soul and the Saviour as long as we are determined to be loyal to Him. The Shulamite encouraged her heart with a threefold thought of her beloved: "My beloved is mine and I am his." She occupied herself with his relationship, more real to her than any family tie. "He feedeth [his flock] among lilies." She thought of his royalty, for the lily is a regally robed flower. "Until the day breaks and the shadows flee away," she occupied herself with dreams of his return. Thoughts such as these fired *her loyalty* to her absent shepherd.

We have the same three weapons with which to fight against the hostility and pressure of the world. Let us think of our Beloved and of His relationship: "My beloved is mine, and I am His."

> Now I belong to Jesus,
>   Jesus belongs to me;
> Not for the years of time alone
>   But for eternity.
>   NORMAN J. CLAYTON

It is a relationship which is unique in the universe. None

of the heavenly hosts know anything like it. Israel knew no such relationship. None of the Old Testament saints came anywhere near it. Not even John the Baptist, of whom Jesus said, "Verily I say unto you, among them that are born of women there hath not risen a greater" (Matthew 11:11)—not even he knew a relationship like this. God has given us a relationship to the Lord Jesus which will be the object of endless astonishment to all the universe through all the ages of an eternity yet to come.

Let us think, too, of our Beloved and His royalty. Who can compare with Him? Did He Himself not say, "a greater than Solomon is here"? His is the true magnificence of the lily. His royalty is far greater than that of a Hebrew king as it unites the majestic office of the king with the ministerial office of the priest.

Let us think, moreover, of His return. The lonely hours of separation are only "Until the day break, and the shadows flee away." That is the great hope of the Church! It is intended to be a purifying hope: "[he] that hath this hope in Him purifieth himself, even as He is pure" (1 John 3:3). Thoughts of His imminent return will help to keep us true to Him and unspotted from the world, no matter what pressures are brought to bear.

The Shulamite tells of her passionate *longing:* "Turn, my beloved, and be thou like a roe or a young hart upon the mountains of Bether" (2:17b). The mountains of Bether are rendered by some as the mountains of separation. "Liken thyself, my beloved, to a gazelle or to a young stag upon the cleft of the mountains" (Rotherham). Darby suggests in his footnote, "cloven mountains" or "mountains full of ravines." The Shulamite saw her beloved as a deer, at home upon those mountains, able to leap over their obstacles. In the Bible, animals of the deer family represent swiftness, beauty, and gentleness. The mountains of separation might stand between them but he was free as a stag or a gazelle, able to come and go at will.

The absence of our Lord should quicken our longing for Him. The mountains of separation have stood solid and silent for nearly two thousand years. It is so long since the word came from the excellent glory: "This same Jesus . . . shall so come in like manner as ye have seen Him go into heaven" (Acts 1:11). We are imprisoned on a rebellious planet in a world of time and space; He inhabits eternity. We are creatures of mortal clay; He is the uncreated, self-existing Son of the living God. But we need to remember that those mountains are nothing to Him. One of these days He will rend the heavens and come down, annihilating all distance, dissolving all time!

2. A Hungry Love (3:1-3)

The Shulamite, still talking to the women of Solomon's court, still recalling the past, tells of *her frantic search:* "By night on my bed I sought him whom my soul loveth: I sought him, but I found him not" (3:1). She had dreamed of her beloved, a dream so real that when she awoke she put out her hand to touch him, but he was not there. It had left her shaken with her heart crying out for the absent one.

Have we ever dreamed that vividly about our heavenly Beloved? The night watches are a wonderful time in which to seek Him in the yearning thoughts of our hearts. When we find that sleep takes its flight, instead of tossing and turning upon our beds, we should quietly compose our thoughts to think of Psalm 23, Isaiah 53, John 10, or some other great passage of Scripture that speaks of Him. We can reach out to Him in the darkness of the night and tell Him how hungry we are for His love.

The Shulamite tells of *her foolish supposition:* "I will rise now, and go about the city in the streets, and in the broad ways I will seek him whom my soul loveth: I sought him, but I found him not" (3:2).

Think what this woman did. She arose from her bed, slipped out into the night alone, and began to explore the dark streets of that eastern city, driven by her heart hunger for her shepherd. It was a foolish thing to do. Had she forgotten that he was a shepherd and that his home was on the distant hills, not in the city? Had she forgotten the dangers that lurk on a city street at night? Her loneliness, her longing, her love drove her into a course of action which was not merely unwise but foolish.

There is nothing the Lord Jesus treasures more than a genuine heart hunger for Himself and the expressions of that love. But the Lord cautions us not to do things which are foolish or which would compromise the testimony. He understands the temptations. Once Satan urged Him to throw Himself down from the pinnacle of the Temple in order to demonstrate the greatness of His trust in God. That kind of thing is not faith but folly.

Grandiose schemes often end in disaster. Their promoters, like Simon Peter in his fleshly enthusiasm on more than one occasion, tend to run ahead of God. It would be possible to cite numerous instances of works which expanded too fast, which branched out into daring ventures which obviously were not in the mind of God, for they collapsed, bringing shame and discredit upon the testimony. There is a fine line between commitment and common sense. One should never do anything without seeking the will of God in diligent prayer, nor act in a way contrary to the known and revealed mind and will of God as set forth in Scripture. God never asks us to act in a way which is contrary to His Word.

Nor does He ask us to act on impulse. We need to remember that when we are contemplating a course of action which calls for a decision. It is the tempter who puts the pressure on, who urges a hurried decision. The great principle to remember when contemplating some bold action for God is the principle of patience: "Wait, I say, on the LORD" (Psalm 27:14).

The Shulamite tells of *her false situation:* "The watchmen that go about the city found me: to whom I said, Saw ye him whom my soul loveth?" (3:3) What would the watchmen think but that she was a woman of the streets? Who else would be parading the streets of a city at night? To be picked up by the city guard put the Shulamite in a very compromising situation. It is a good thing the Lord sometimes rescues us from the consequences of our own folly.

3. A Hallowed Love (3:4-5)

Heart delight (3:4): The Shulamite then *saw her beloved.* The story does not tell us how or why he happened to be there, but he was, just when she needed him most.

How wonderful! The Lord always reveals Himself to those who truly love Him. He has His own inimitable way of making His presence felt, of drawing close to us to comfort and cheer, just when we need Him most.

The Shulamite *seized her beloved:* "I found him whom my soul loveth: I held him, and would not let him go." Can we not picture the scene? We can see her clinging to him, sobbing out her love, telling him in broken sentences all that had happened.

It is all so true to life. We see Mary Magdalene alone in the garden on the resurrection morn, staring forlornly at the empty tomb. Then suddenly she heard a sound and wheeled around to see, in the glory of the morn, a man standing there. She thought it was the gardener, it must have been he who had removed the body! She begged him to tell her where it had been hidden. Then the stranger spoke a word, just one, "Mary!" In that moment she knew Him, it was the Lord. She flung her arms around Him crying, "Master!" Gently He disengaged Himself from her hold, "Touch Me not, detain Me not," He said (John 20:16-17). She would have held on to Him forever. "I have found him whom my soul loveth: I held him, and would not let him go."

Do we ever feel like that toward the Lord? Do the floodtides of emotion ever rise to overflowing in our soul so that we would like to cling to Him and hold Him forever to our heart?

The Shulamite *showed her beloved:* "I held him, and would not let him go, until I had brought him into my mother's house, and into the chamber of her that conceived me" (3:4). The Shulamite brought this dear shepherd of hers into the home where her brothers lived. She did not introduce him to them yet, she would get her mother to know and love him first.

Perhaps it is not always the mother whose heart is most ready, but the Shulamite had the right idea. What a great thing it is when a newly saved person is able to introduce the Lord Jesus to someone at home! May we ever be quick to unveil the Lord Jesus. May we so live that, in the inner recesses of our home, where our nearest and our dearest dwell, Christ may truly be seen.

Heart danger (3:5): "I charge you, O ye daughters of

Jerusalem, by the roes and by the hinds of the field, that ye stir not up, nor awake my love, till he please" (3:5). Three times the Shulamite has to repeat this warning to the court women. The "daughters of Jerusalem" sought to incite her and were *the source* of the danger. They were Solomon's women, in love with what he had to offer, amused at the Shulamite's single-minded devotion to a mere shepherd. There are always those who will try to tempt the believer away from loyalty to Christ.

The substance of the danger is equally evident. The Shulamite adjures these women, by "the roes and the hinds of the field," by all that was free, by all that spoke of her beloved, not to awaken her love "till he please." If we retain the personal, masculine pronoun, then she was simply telling these women that her hallowed love was reserved for her shepherd and to leave her alone.

The scene and the subject change with the next verse. We leave the Shulamite resolutely true to her shepherd, gladly speaking of him even to those who would tempt her into unfaithfulness. Surely we shall take our stand with her, sold out completely to the Shepherd of our souls, our love reserved first and foremost for Him.

V. AN HOUR OF TALK

Song of Solomon 3:6-11

SOLOMON TRIUMPHANTLY enters Jerusalem and the streets of the city are lined with a cheering, admiring throng. The world welcomes its own by praising, as in Solomon's case, the things it most admires. Here Solomon is unlike Christ, the meek and lowly Jesus, who rode into Jerusalem on an ass's colt.

The Bible has much to tell us about the world and its ways and attitudes towards the things of God: "If any man love the world, the love of the Father is not in him" (1 John 2:15). That does not mean the material world—the world of grass and flowers, of rivers, seas, and shores, of meadows and mountains, forests and farms, but the *moral* world; a system of human life and society as it is organized and propagated as the enemy of God. John sums it up as "the lust of the flesh, and the lust of the eyes, and the pride of life" (1 John 2:16).

The people who line the streets in this section of the song, and those who speak out with typical worldly comments know nothing about the shepherd and his beloved Shulamite.

The world, after all, is not interested in Christ and His true Bride, the spiritual Church. The outward, the visible, the spectacular, the material are the things the multitudes

admire. Spiritual, mystical, and other worldly things have
no attraction for them.

A. THE WORLD AND ITS POMP (3:6)

1. The Sophisticated

"Who is this that cometh out of the wilderness?" Or,
perhaps more literally, "What is this that cometh out of the
wilderness?" Evidently the speaker is astonished. The wilderness was the last place from which he could expect to
see emerging such an entourage as this.

Solomon had been to the backwoods only for a visit.
Country living, that which is simple and natural, had no
lasting appeal for him. He might study the world of nature
and write books about the things of the countryside but big
cities are the very essence of human sophistication.

Originally, God placed man in a garden and blessed him
with a simple and beautiful life. After the fall, Cain put man
in a city. No sooner is the city introduced in Scripture than
the Spirit of God begins to talk of man's scientific develop-
ments, his artistic accomplishments, his engineering potential, his increasingly sophisticated methods of marketing
and merchandising, the movement of society towards per-
missiveness (Genesis 4).

Solomon is seen coming out of the wilderness, out of the
country, away from the natural and simple, back to the
city, back to the sophisticated and artificial.

2. The Spectacular

"Who is this that cometh out of the wilderness like
pillars of smoke?" A column of smoke towers above every-

thing else, it catches the eye, causes instant comment, and gives rise to speculation. A pillar of smoke is born of the fire—it is black, ugly, menacing, a sign that something is burning.

Solomon was like that pillar of smoke. He did everything in a grand way. He drew and held the eye, he dominated everything. But nobody, surveying the long-range effects of his life, would say that his extravagances were beneficial. Even his own people turned against him in the end, sick and tired of his taxes, his orientalism, and his apostasies.

3. The Sensational

"Who is this that cometh . . . perfumed with myrrh and frankincense?" Myrrh and frankincense are two powerful spices that seize upon the senses and hold them enthralled. The myrrh had a social significance in Bible times, for weddings and for funerals, the gladdest and saddest hours of life. The frankincense had a sacred use in religious ceremonies. It was one of the gifts brought by the wise men to Jesus at the time of his birth.

Solomon was perfumed with myrrh and frankincense, a reminder of his presence and of his control in every phase of his people's lives.

4. The Seductive

"Who is this that cometh . . . with all powders of the merchant?" (3:6) The powders of the merchant suggest sensuality for sale. "Who is this?" is in the feminine. The rest of the passage clearly refers to Solomon so the use of the feminine must be taken as a reference to Solomon's taste for oriental luxury and sensual indulgence.

All that was sophisticated, sensational, spectacular, and seductive is thus associated with Solomon by the first of the four speakers who comment on Solomon's parade.

B. THE WORLD AND ITS POWER (3:7-8)

"Behold his bed [his couch, or his sedan chair], which is Solomon's; threescore valiant men are about it, of the valiant of Israel. They all hold swords, being expert in war: every man hath his sword upon his thigh because of fear in the night." The whole emphasis is on the world and its power.

1. Solomon's Style (3:7a)

"Behold his [sedan chair] which is Solomon's." Solomon was coming into the city like an oriental despot and the world applauded him for thus ministering to its own ideas about the way rank, power, and privilege should enjoy and flaunt itself.

2. Solomon's Strength (3:7b-8)

The world is always impressed by a show of strength. It despises weakness and has agreed with Charles Darwin, in his *Origin of the Species,* that "might is right," the weak have no right to survive, only the fit and strong should inherit the earth.

Had the Lord Jesus, at His first coming, descended from the sky with the armies of Heaven at His back, had he reduced Rome to rubble and used His power to annihilate the legions of Caesar, then the Jews and the world would have hailed Him as a conquering King of kings. When He fed five thousand hungry men with loaves and fishes, marvelously multiplied from the scant supply of a little lad's lunch, at once they wanted to crown Him king, even against His will. This world is always impressed by the martial and the material.

We are not surprised, therefore, that Solomon, as a type of this world's prince, won his applause by a display of power and might. The crowds lining the way as Solomon's mighty men marched in battle array were impressed by Solomon's *warriors:* "Threescore valiant men are about it [the sedan chair], of the valiant of Israel" (3:7), they exclaimed.

The *weapons:* "Every man hath his sword upon his thigh because of fear in the night." These were trained troops that kept pace with Solomon's entourage, men hardened to war, ready to protect their sovereign by their swords. The whole display mirrors for us the world and its power, centered around a parade of marching men armed to the teeth and ready for war.

C. THE WORLD AND ITS PROSPERITY (3:9-10)

"King Solomon made himself a chariot of the wood of Lebanon. He made the pillars thereof of silver, the bottom thereof of gold, the covering of it of purple, the midst thereof being paved with love, for the daughters of Jerusalem."

Here was a tribute to the purchasing power of money, one of the gods of this world—what Jesus called the "mammon of unrighteousness." Solomon's income, in gold, amounted to six hundred sixty-six talents;[1] he had so much wealth that even the pots and pans in his kitchen were made of gold (1 Kings 10:14-21). Certainly those watching Solomon's magnificent entry into the city were impressed with his display of wealth. The world is always impressed with financial success. Money can buy *excellence.* "King Solomon made himself a chariot of the wood of Lebanon." The costly cedar of Lebanon had a magnificent grain, rich and elegant when planed and polished. Cedar is an aromatic wood much prized even today for chests in which blankets and linens can be kept free from moths. Solomon built the temple and his royal palace out of cedar. Its wood was not for the poor but for the powerful rich.

"He made the pillars thereof of silver, the bottom thereof of gold." No base metals for Solomon! Nothing but silver and gold. The world may criticize *extravagance* but that is usually because they covet it.

"The covering of it of purple, the midst thereof being paved with love, for the daughters of Jerusalem." His couch was "covered in purple," which suggests all that is royal. It was "paved with love by the daughters of Jerusalem" (as Darby renders the phrase), which suggests all that is romantic.

D. THE WORLD AND ITS POPULARITY (3:11)

1. The Shallow Crowd

"Go forth, O ye daughters of Zion, and behold king

---

[1]A talent is about 1200 ounces. With the price of gold fluctuating between $500 and $600 an ounce, Solomon's annual income would average about $444,000,000 a year.

Solomon with the crown." The expression, "daughters of Zion," occurs here and in two passages of Isaiah. When Isaiah employs the phrase he uses it as an expression of contempt: "Because the daughters of Zion are haughty, and walk with stretched forth necks and wanton eyes, walking and mincing as they go, and making a tinkling with their feet: Therefore the Lord will smite with a scab the crown of the head of the daughters of Zion, and the LORD will discover their secret parts" (Isaiah 3:16-17). Later, anticipating the day when the Lord will restore Israel to her proper place among the nations, Isaiah says that this happy occasion will be "when the Lord shall have washed away the filth of the daughters of Zion" (Isaiah 4:4).

The Holy Spirit uses the phrase to depict Israel in her brazen, immodest, and flaunting form. If the phrase is used consistently, then, in the song, it must refer to women of doubtful morals. The worldly, shallow crowd, shouting Solomon's praise, could see nothing wrong with these "daughters of Zion" going forth to meet Solomon. On the contrary, they applauded them.

2. The Shallow Crown

"Behold king Solomon with the crown wherewith his mother crowned him in the day of his espousals [*the day of his marriage*], and in the day of the gladness of his heart" (4:11b). Solomon was married amid scenes of pomp and pageantry, to the daughter of Pharaoh, king of Egypt. Marriage with an Egyptian was just the kind of worldly marriage that appealed to Solomon's political instincts— for him, as Israel's king, to cement an alliance by marriage with powerful, magnificent Egypt (frequently used in the Scripture as a picture of the world)!

It was *the day of Solomon's merriment,* but whatever gladness he might have found in this worldly marriage soon evaporated as he sought his happiness elsewhere. He is doing the same thing here by trying to seduce the Shulamite from her pledged love and loyalty to her shepherd. But the Shulamite wants no part in Solomon at all. All she wants is her own beloved.

So it should be with us. The world is all about us, freely expressing its own sense of values. Paul tells us we should evaluate the world in the light of the cross: "by whom the world is crucified unto me, and I unto the world" (Galatians 6:14).

> Nay, world, I turn away,
>   Though thou seem fair and good;
> That friendly, outstretched hand of thine
>   Is stained with Jesus' blood.

VI. AN HOUR OF TRYST

Song of Solomon 4:1 — 5:1

IN THIS SECTION of the song the shepherd once more tells his beloved Shulamite how greatly he loves her and assures her that, when the time is ripe, he will be ready to come and carry her away from all the dangers and temptations which beset her now. In this lovely section the shepherd and the Shulamite converse together.

We see in this delightful dialogue the love relationship which exists between Christ and His Church. This hour of tryst, recorded in such detail, is surely intended to teach us how we should talk to our Shepherd and also to show us how He communicates with us.

There are four major steps in the Shulamite's story here. We have her personal radiance, her passionate response, her pilgrim responsibilities, and her promised rapture. We shall be exploring something of the height and depth, the length and breadth of the love of Christ that passes knowledge and the occasional heart response of the believer to that astonishing love of His.

A. THE PERSONAL RADIANCE OF THE SHULAMITE (4:1-5)

Notice the marked contrast between the shepherd's words and Solomon's coarse flatteries. We are not told how the shepherd was able to be alone with the Shulamite but love has its own ways to circumvent difficulties and hindrances and to keep its rendezvous. And we know there is no power in heaven, earth, or hell which can prevent Christ and the believer from having their hour of tryst.

1. The Exclamation of the Shepherd (4:1a)

"Behold, thou art fair; my love; behold, thou art fair."
"Lo, thou art beautiful, my fair one. Lo! thou art beautiful" (Rotherham).

The Lord looks upon His Church and sees us without spot or blemish (Ephesians 5:27), in the beauty and perfection which will be ours when, in that rapturous moment, we see Him as He is and are instantly changed into His likeness. Love exclaims, "Thou art fair, my dear, so fair!" Obviously Christ sees in us something we cannot see in ourselves.

2. The Explanation of the Shepherd (4:1b-5)

The shepherd explains in loving detail what he sees when he gazes upon his Shulamite. He describes seven features about her which thrill his heart in order to draw out her response.

He mentions *her mystery:* "Thou hast doves' eyes within thy locks" (4:1b), "Thine eyes are doves' from behind thy veil" (Rotherham).

Eastern women customarily went out veiled as an act of modesty, to hide their faces from the curious eyes of men. The eyes of a woman, seen behind a gauzy veil, are mysterious. The eye is the most expressive member of the human body, sometimes called "the mirror of the soul," reflecting the secrets of the heart. To know what another person is thinking we need only watch that person's face, particularly his eyes. The shifty eye reveals deceit, the glaring eye anger, the tear-filled eye sorrow, the dancing eye mischief, the soulful eye love.

The shepherd describes his beloved's eyes as dove's eyes. The commanding eye of a dove is perfectly round and is the most prominent feature on its face.

The dove is the Biblical symbol for the Holy Spirit. As Christ looks at His Church, as He looks at us, what catches and holds His eye is the joy of seeing the Holy Spirit indwelling the believer and so expressing Himself through the believer's personality that his very eye is affected. How wonderful it would be if, every time the Lord Jesus looked at us, He could see that wonderful Holy Spirit of love, joy, peace, grace, truth, wisdom, faith, and power shining out of our eyes.

The Shulamite's majesty: "Thy hair is as a flock of goats, that appear from Mount Gilead" (4:1c). Gilead was a beautiful part of Palestine, a region famous for its rolling hills and green pastures. The shepherd likens his beloved's long, flowing locks to goats streaming down one of the Gilead hills.

In the Word of God a woman's hair is the symbol of her glory and of the special majesty with which God has crowned her (1 Corinthians 11:14-15). What the Lord Jesus wants to see in us is a display of the majesty He has conferred upon each believer. We are betrothed to Heaven's Beloved. He has bestowed upon us a majesty beyond that given to any other creature. As a woman's hair is her glory, so we should display by our character, conduct, and conversation the majesty and glory which are ours.

The Shulamite's magnificence: "Thy teeth are like a flock

of sheep that are even shorn, which came up from the washing; whereof every one bear twins, and none is barren among them" (4:2). If there is one feature of the face which can mar the beauty of an otherwise attractive countenance it is the teeth. In earlier times, and even today in less fortunate lands, teeth were often crooked. They rapidly decayed, turned yellow, and fell out leaving ugly gaps and allowing cheeks to cave in. People became prematurely old and wizened-looking. To have beautiful white teeth was a rare magnificence in either a woman or a man.

The Shulamite's teeth were perfect. There was nothing to mar her smile. Is there anything that mars ours? One of the great beauties of the believer should be his smile, a smile born of the welling joy within, expressed at all times and in all circumstances.

Joy is much deeper than mere happiness. Happiness depends on what happens, joy is the fruit of the Spirit. One thing which can mar our joy is for us to grieve the Holy Spirit. As the great Shepherd of the sheep looks upon His chosen Bride, He wants her to smile back into His face with an unspoiled smile, made perfect by the indwelling Spirit's overflowing joy.

The Shulamite's mouth: "Thy lips are like a thread of scarlet, and thy speech is comely" (4:3a). "Like a cord of crimson are thy lips, and thy mouth is lovely" (Rotherham). The human mouth, like the human eye, is an expressive part of the face. It can register hardness or tenderness, sorrow or mirth, pain or surprise, humor or horror. We only have to think of the ease with which an artist, having drawn a face with its nose and ears and eyes and eyebrows, can change its whole expression by turning the corners of the mouth either up or down.

The shepherd looks at his beloved's mouth and his soul

finds its satisfaction in the tender truths formed and framed just for his ears.

Where, in all this wide world today, can the Lord Jesus find words to fill His loving heart with joy, unless those words come from the lips of His own? Nobody else can speak the language of Zion, nobody else has a mouth capable of expressing the thoughts He wants to hear. Our beloved Lord listens to the babble of noise that ascends on high from this earth in a thousand tongues. He is listening for those who speak His language, the language of Heaven. He is listening for someone who will say from the heart:

> My Jesus, I love Thee, I know Thou art mine,
> For Thee all the follies of sin I resign;
> My gracious Redeemer, my Saviour art Thou!
> If ever I loved Thee, Lord Jesus 'tis now.
>
> I love Thee because Thou hast first loved me,
> And purchased my pardon on Calvary's tree
> I love Thee for wearing the thorns on Thy brow,
> If ever I loved Thee, Lord Jesus 'tis now.
>
> A. J. GORDON

His instant response will be, "Like a cord of crimson are thy lips, and thy mouth is lovely."

The shepherd mentions *the Shulamite's modesty:* "Thy temples are like a piece of pomegranate within thy locks" (4:3b). "Like a slice of pomegranate are thy temples behind thy veil" (Rotherham). Some versions, such as Darby, render the word "temples" as "cheeks."

The pomegranate looks something like an apple on the outside but when it is sliced, the inside appears a brilliant red. Possibly, as the shepherd tells his beloved Shulamite what beauty he sees in her, her cheeks and temples blush

crimson as she reddens with modesty. That too delights
the shepherd for it means that the one he loves is pure as
the breaking of the day when the sky blushes red at the
appearance of the sun. So too the Lord intends His Church
to present a modest profile to the world. He admires His
bride when she modestly attends to her duties and engages
her affections to Him in selfless love.

Fittingly, the shepherd next makes mention of *the
Shulamite's might:* "Thy neck is like the tower of David
builded for an armory, whereon hang a thousand bucklers,
all shields of mighty men" (4:4). The shepherd saw around
the neck of his beloved a string of coins, such as eastern
women wore to symbolize betrothal. Certainly a string of
such coins around the neck, shining in the sun, would look
like an array of shields hung on the wall of an armory.

In Bible times marriages were arranged. As soon as the
assent of the bride's parents was obtained, the suitor gave
the bride a betrothal gift. The bride-to-be wore this gift to
act as a protection. The coins, like the engagement ring of
today, warned other would-be suitors that her heart and
her hand have been pledged to another. Unwanted or
improper advances can thus be warded off.

It would seem that the shepherd had already given his
beloved shepherdess this pledge of affection and intent
and that she wore the coins about her neck. Solomon, in
his approaches to the Shulamite, obviously ignored the
token coins. Yet, as we have seen, he did not dare to
tamper with her though he was king. The laws of God and
the conventions of society would have condemned him.
The Shulamite, to that extent, was protected by her shining string of coins.

Our great Shepherd's betrothal gift to His Bride is the
Holy Spirit. He is called "the earnest of our inheritance"

(Ephesians 1:14). The thought behind that word "earnest" is exactly the thought behind the idea of an engagement ring. We are to display the Holy Spirit before the world to signify that our affections have been engaged to another, "even to Him who is raised from the dead" (Romans 7:4).

The shepherd remarks on *the Shulamite's maturity:* "Thy two breasts are like two young roes that are twins, which feed among the lilies" (4:5). He sees her noble shape, carefully veiled behind the long tresses of her hair and the flowing contours of her veil—a mature, grown woman.

Full development does not come all at once. It takes time to bring out the beauty of the flower, to grow a tree, to ripen a young girl into a mature and marriageable young woman. God is never in a hurry whether it be in nature or in grace.

It seems such a very long time since the Lord Jesus went home to glory, such a long time since the Church was introduced into this world. The Holy Spirit has been at work in the intervening years, however, patiently bringing the Church to maturity. The eternal purposes of God in the Church have been allowed to ripen with what seems, to us, maddening slowness, but soon now the Church will be fully mature and ready for the glory.

B. The Passionate Response of the Shulamite (4:6)

The Shulamite responds to her shepherd speaking about the morning and the mountain.

1. The Morning—What A Fantastic Morning It Will Be

"Until the day break, and the shadows flee away." Her

heart is occupied with the coming day. Right now Solomon has her in his gilded prison, but he cannot keep her there forever nor can he harm her so long as her heart remains true to her beloved. One day the shadows will flee away and the bright and blessed day will dawn. That is her hope, and that is the great hope of the Church.

> On that bright and golden morning
>   when the Son of man shall come,
> And the radiance of His glory we shall see;
> When from every clime and nation
>   He shall call His people home,
> What a gathering of the ransomed that will be!
>   FANNY J. CROSBY

2. The Mountain—What A Fragrant Mountain It Will Be

"I will get me to the mountain of myrrh, and to the hill of frankincense." No such mountain exists on earth, this is part of the landscape of Heaven.

The myrrh and frankincense were two of the gifts brought so long ago by the wise men and presented to the infant Christ in the place where the guiding star led them. They are gifts we associate with the Lord's death on the cross of Calvary, and also with His high-priestly work in the glory now being carried on for us who are still down here amid the shadows. One day we shall breathe forever the fragrance of the myrrh and the frankincense. Their perfume will bring back fond reminders of His love for us in the days when the shadows still lingered over our lives.

C. THE PILGRIM RESPONSIBILITIES OF THE SHULAMITE (4:7-15)

The shepherd is aware of the dangers and temptations which surround the beloved in Solomon's licentious court. He is concerned with the possibility that she might eventually succumb to the seductive sensualities with which she is surrounded. She must not forget her shepherd!

The world's chief weapons against the Church are the same as those employed by Solomon—fear and flattery. We live in a world of time and sense. The emphasis is on those things which are seen and temporal. Since it is eternity that really counts the great Lover of our souls would have us remember where we are and whose we are. Like the shepherd in the song, the Lord seeks to get us alone with Himself in order to remind us afresh of these things and to assure us once again of His love.

The shepherd talks to the Shulamite about her person, position, passion, protection, and perfections. If we allow our Shepherd to bring these same realities home to our hearts, we too will be fortified against the wiles and the wickedness of the evil one, against the world over which he reigns, and against the inbred treacheries of our own wayward hearts.

1. Her Person (4:7)

"Thou art all fair, my love; there is no spot in thee." The shepherd looks at the Shulamite with the eyes of love. He sees the spotless beauty and perfection love always sees in the beloved. The powerful magnetic forces of attraction often work in these mysterious levels of the subconscious where the ordinary rules of rationality are set aside.

Christ sees His Church, His Bride, with no blemish in her at all. He sees her, not as she appears now, in this world of sin, but as she will be in that glorious day when she will be presented to the universe on high—His blood-bought, blood-washed Church, "without spot or wrinkle or any such thing" (Ephesians 5:27)—His Bride. Every eye will be turned upon us and, wonder of wonders, we shall be fair as the morning, the most beautiful, magnificent vision of loveliness ever to dawn upon a created being's eyes, for we shall be like Him!

> And is it so—I shall be like Thy Son?
> Is this the grace which He for me has won?
> Father of glory! (thought beyond all thought!)
> In glory, to His own blest likeness brought!
>
> Yet it must be: Thy love had not its rest
> Were Thy redeemed not with Thee fully blest.
> That love that gives not as the world, but shares
> All it possesses with its loved coheirs.
>   JOHN NELSON DARBY

In that day, we shall be beautiful beyond compare and He will truly say, "Thou art all fair, my love; there is no spot in thee."

2. Her Position (4:8)

"Come with me from Lebanon, my spouse, with me from Lebanon: look from the top of Amana, from the top of Shenir and Hermon, from the lions' dens, from the mountains of the leopards."

The shepherd realizes, even more than the Shulamite, what a dangerous place she is in. For the time, she is a prisoner and cannot physically transport herself from her surroundings. However, her spirit is free to soar to other realms. So the wise shepherd talks to the Shulamite about *the peaks to be climbed:* "Come with me from Lebanon, my spouse, with me from Lebanon: look from the top of Amana, from the top of Shenir and Hermon." The shepherd is doing with the Shulamite what our Lord is doing with us, seeking to set her affections on things above! He is urging her, in spite of her present restrictions, to plant her feet by faith on higher ground: "Yes, I know where you are. I know the perils of that gilded cage. But just think of me, for where I am there shall you be also. Think of me on the heights. That is how to triumph over the world, the flesh, and the tempter there in that palace prison of yours."

The significance of those places named by the shepherd, these peaks to be climbed spiritually by faith, will help us to appreciate the wisdom of the shepherd.

The name Lebanon means "whiteness." It was the poetic name given to the snow-clad heights of Hermon which stand out in dazzling brightness against the skyline of the Holy Land. In speaking of Lebanon, the shepherd referred to the character of his beloved. Like himself, she was destined for those snow-covered heights.

Amana means "constancy," "integrity," "truth,"—one lexicon suggests "a covenant"—different shades of the same basic idea. Amana is the mountain from which the river Abana flows. When Naaman the leper was told by Elisha to go and wash in Jordan he bristled at once. "Are not Abana and Pharpar, rivers of Damascus, better than all the waters of Israel?" (2 Kings 5:12) He was thinking of those everflowing streams that came down from Amana. The name Amana would suggest thoughts of constancy to the Shulamite. She must remember the covenant between them.

Shenir was the Amorite name for Mount Hermon, meaning "bear the lamp," "pointed," or "peak." The name was a poetical reminder to the Shulamite of her confession, for she was to bear the lamp, to stand firm and resolute like a mountain peak.

Hermon means "devoted" or "sacred mountain." Hermon is the highest mountain in or around the Holy Land. The Canaanites had their sacred places on its lofty slopes. The name would suggest to the Shulamite her commitment, for she was not her own, she was his.

What a wonderful association of ideas for us to hold to our hearts in this dark world of sin: our character, to keep it as white as the snows of Lebanon; our constancy, the covenant relationship of our betrothal to our Lord; our confession, as lights in this dark world and as a city set on a hill we cannot be hid; and our commitment, our pledge to our Shepherd!

The shepherd reminds the Shulamite of *the perils to be considered.* He is a realist and knows that she needs to be aware of the dangers of her position because human nature is such that we quickly accustom ourselves to our environment. "Come," says the shepherd, "come from the lions' dens, from the mountains of the leopards." She was in enemy territory and the enemy was there as a lion, the king of beasts; and as a leopard, the most beautiful of beasts. The enemy was dangerous—would rend, tear, and destroy. But she could overcome amid the dangers of her environment by looking within and cultivating her love for her shepherd daily.

3. Her Passion (4:9-11)

The shepherd tells his beloved that her love is beyond anything he has ever known, beyond compulsion, comparison, and comprehension. That is how the Lord evaluates our love for Him. He treasures each thought of love we have or express for Him even though these thoughts, in themselves, might be weak and poor.

> Weak is the effort of our heart,
> And cold our warmest thought;
> But when we see Thee as Thou art
> We'll praise Thee as we ought.
> JOHN NEWTON

Our Lord knows that, but He treasures each expression of love as being more precious to Him than gold. How wonderful He is when we consider how meager, inadequate, and infrequent are our expressions of love for Him. How humbling it is that He should love us so!

The shepherd senses that the Shulamite's love is *beyond compulsion:* "Thou hast ravished my heart, my sister, my spouse; thou hast ravished my heart with one of thine eyes [Rotherham—with one glance of thine eyes], with one chain of thy neck" (4:9).

Love has its own language and often it is the language of looks. It cannot be commanded, it comes from within, it is beyond compulsion.

"Thou shalt love the LORD thy God with all thine heart . . . and thy neighbour as thyself," wrote Moses into the law (Deuteronomy 6:5; Leviticus 19:18). It doesn't work. In the New Testament all this is changed and everything is lifted to higher ground: "God commandeth His love

toward us, in that, while we were yet sinners, Christ died for us" (Romans 5:8). In the Old Testament our love for God is commanded, in the New Testament His love for us is commended. The heart of the believer is suddenly taken up with the person and the passion of the Shepherd and love shines out of the eyes and shows up in the life as a result. When it is there, there is a distinctive turning toward Him in all the affairs of life.

The shepherd says that the Shulamite's love is *beyond comparison:* "How fair is thy love, my sister, my spouse! how much better is thy love than wine! and the smell of thine ointments than all spices!" (4:10) Their relationship is one of purity for he calls her "my sister." It is also one of passion for he calls her "my spouse" or, in today's language, "my bride." Her love is better than wine, it is to be savored; better than ointments and spices, it is to be sensed. There are probably no greater stimulants to passion than wine and perfume. However, until their passion can be indulged in the marriage relationship, he loves her as a sister. He loves her passionately but purely.

That, too, is how Christ loves the Church. His love for us has all the purity of a family relationship and all the potential of a future relationship. The love between Christ and His Church is so sacred that human language can hardly express it. It thrills Him now, and He looks forward to the day when our love can be brought to its full flower and eternal potential in Heaven.

The Shulamite's love is *beyond comprehension:* "Thy lips, O my spouse, drop as the honeycomb: honey and milk are under thy tongue; and the smell of thy garments is like the smell of Lebanon" (4:11). Her love is so sweet it could only be compared with honey, so satisfying it is like honey and milk. Her love is so stimulating it is like Lebanon, which yields the fragrant and beautiful cedar.

All this is but an echo, in a sweet, ancient song, of what the Lord Jesus thinks of our love for Him! We should be ashamed that we do not love Him more and that we do not tell Him of our love more often.

4. Her Protection (4:12)

"A garden inclosed is my sister, my spouse; a spring shut up, a fountain sealed." The shepherd reiterates the relationship in which he holds her—sister and spouse.

Her exotic beauty, as a garden, is enclosed. *Her exhaustless bounty,* as a spring shut up, has its bounds. *Her exuberant behavior,* as a fountain, is effervescent, bubbling, overflowing. No wonder people were attracted to her! But the shepherd must always come first; anything that would trespass upon his claim is forbidden. The Shulamite's protection lies in remembering that.

The Lord looks upon His Church with an equally jealous eye. The Church is a garden, a spring, a fountain, everything that is delightful and desirable and dynamic. It is no wonder that the great enemy of the souls, who knows the tremendous potential of the Church, desires to seduce it and seize its influence for himself. He would like to see its love for Christ denied, its testimony ruined, its effectiveness neutralized. He never ceases working toward this end.

But we have protection against his wiles. Satan can tempt but he cannot seduce, he can offer but he cannot force. The ultimate choice is ours. We are protected, ultimately, by a will wholly yielded to the will of our Beloved.

5. Her Perfections (4:13-15)

The shepherd finds the Shulamite *superlatively fruitful:*

"Thy plants are an orchard of pomegranates, with pleasant fruits" (4:13a). The word translated orchards carries
with it the idea of "a paradise." Darby translates it: "Thy
shoots are a paradise of pomegranates."

Eastern monarchs built parks around their palaces. They
were places of delight—shady, fragrant, filled with everything which would appeal to a sense of beauty and enjoy-
ment. Often these paradises stood in marked contrast with
the stark, sandy, or rocky terrain of the surrounding dis-
trict. Pomegranate trees were common in such orchards.
The pomegranate, a Biblical symbol for fruitfulness, contains a very large number of luscious, pulpy, red seeds.

The Shulamite seemed a fruitful paradise in contrast
with everything else the world could offer. That is exactly
what the Lord Jesus sees in us! He, who has all the angels
of glory to hang upon His Word and rush to do His bidding, sets His love supremely on us.

"Camphire, with spikenard, spikenard and saffron; cala-
mus and cinnamon, with all trees of frankincense; myrrh
and aloes, with all the chief spices" (4:13b-14). Our senses
are assailed by a bewildering blend of fragrances. Such was
the Shulamite to the shepherd, *superlatively fragrant.* Everything about her breathed an air of loveliness yet each is
distinct in itself.

Our Lord would like to have us shed abroad the many
fragrances of a Spirit-filled personality so that now grace
and truth and joy and peace and faith and kindness and
all these separately and together ascend to Him. Such
spiritual perfume will make us lovely to be near, even to
those around us in this polluted world.

"A fountain of gardens [literally, a garden fountain], a
well of living waters, and streams from Lebanon" (4:15).
A fountain, a well, a river! The shepherd saw his beloved

as *superlatively fair,* with infinite sources of refreshment. Only one who has dwelt in the thirsty lands of the Middle East can appreciate those figures. They speak of verdant pastures, of ripening fields of corn, of fruit and flowers, of growing orchards, of everything that can make a barren prospect fair.

In the Old Testament, God the Father is likened to a fountain of living water: "My people have committed two evils; they have forsaken Me the fountain of living waters, and hewed them out cisterns, broken cisterns, that can hold no water" (Jeremiah 2:13). God the Son is a well of living water. To the woman of Sychar He said, "Whosoever drinketh of this water shall thirst again: but whosoever drinketh of the water that I shall give him shall never thirst; but the water that I shall give him shall be in him a well of living water springing up into everlasting life" (John 4:13-14). God the Spirit is a river of living water. "In the last day, that great day of the feast, Jesus stood and cried, saying, If any man thirst, let him come unto Me, and drink. He that believeth on Me, as the Scripture hath said, out of his belly shall flow rivers of living water" (John 7:37-38). As our Lord looks at us, He sees the wonders of the triune God reflected in us, flowing into us, through us, and out of us to a needy, parched, and thirsty world.

The hour of tryst is soon to end but before he leaves the shepherd whispers to his beloved a few words about the greatest and brightest hope of all.

D. THE PROMISED RAPTURE OF THE SHULAMITE
(4:16—5:1)

The Shulamite answers, in a word or two, this outpouring of love on the part of the shepherd. The words he then

speaks are the last he utters to her before he comes again
to receive her to himself. It is interesting, and true to type,
that the Shulamite's words and responses are so much
shorter and less magnificent than the shepherd's. Our Shepherd always seems to have so much more to say to us than
we ever say to Him, and His outpouring for us is always
so much richer, fuller, and deeper than our feeble responses to Him. Our neglected prayer life is sad testimony
to that.

1. The Shulamite's Plea (4:16)

"Awake, O north wind; and come, thou south; blow
upon my garden, that the spices thereof may flow out. Let
my beloved come into his garden, and eat his pleasant
fruits."

The Shulamite's constant desire is to be a blessing. Let the
wind—north or south—blow and they will serve her purpose to minister to the world around her, carrying her
fragrant influences abroad.

In other words, no matter what her circumstances, she
resolves to be a blessing. That is what the shepherd's words
had done for her. That, too, is what our Shepherd's words
can do for us. If we are occupied with Him and His Word,
then come what may, north wind or south wind, adversity
or advancement, bitter trial or blessed experience, winter
snow or summer sun, all shall be made to minister to our
beneficial outreach to those around us.

The Shulamite's consummate desire was the coming again of
her beloved: "Let my beloved come into his garden, and
eat his pleasant fruits." She says, in effect, "Ah! you have
been telling me that I am a garden of delights, a pomegranate paradise, a lovely park in a wilderness world. Well,
beloved, I am all yours."

I am Thine, O Lord, I have heard Thy voice
And it told Thy love to me;
But I long to rise in the arms of faith
And be closer drawn to Thee.

FANNY J. CROSBY

Surely the heart's cry of the believer, overwhelmed with the love of the Saviour, is: "Come, Lord Jesus! I am Yours! Take me to Yourself! Even so, come Lord Jesus." And what will our Beloved say to that? This section of the song tells us.

2. The Shepherd's Pledge (5:1)

It is a pity that, when our Bible was divided up into chapters, chapter 4 was made to end with verse 16 instead of also including verse 1 of chapter 5. The heart of the shepherd is just as excited with the prospect of rapture as is the heart of the Shulamite. He says at once, "I am come [literally, I am coming] into my garden, my sister, my spouse."

The shepherd's great expectation, like that of the Lord Jesus, is that of *marital bliss.*

The first great truth here is that of rapture. The Lord is coming for His Church. He does intend to catch it up into His arms and take it to be forever with Himself. He says, "I go to prepare a place for you. And if I go and prepare a place for you, I will come again, and receive you unto Myself; that where I am, there ye may be also" (John 14:2-3). Under the symbol of marriage the Lord constantly sets before us the bliss we are going to enjoy with Him in a coming eternity. More than that we cannot say. After all, nobody speaks much about the honeymoon! Some moments are too sacred to be shared with anyone but the beloved.

There is also an expectation here of *millenial bliss:* "I have gathered my myrrh with my spice; I have eaten my honey-comb with my honey; I have drunk my wine with my milk." Notice that all the verbs are in the past tense. The spiritual lessons locked up in this statement are profound and blessed, but to extract their full force we have to carry them far beyond the experience and expectation of the Shulamite's shepherd to that of our Shepherd.

"I have gathered my myrrh with my spice." What can this mean but the glory of His sufferings? Never will those sufferings be forgotten. The hymnwriter beautifully refers to the wounds of the Lord Jesus as "rich wounds, yet visible above, in beauty glorified." And so they are.

"I have eaten my honeycomb with my honey." What can this mean but the glory of His sweetness? Who in all the universe is sweeter than the Lord Jesus Christ?

Every day with Jesus is sweeter than the day before,
Every day with Jesus, I love Him more and more;
Jesus saves and keeps me, and He's the One I'm waiting for,
Every day with Jesus is sweeter than the day before.
                                        ROBERT C. LOVELESS

No wonder the Psalmist could exclaim, "O taste and see that the LORD is good" (Psalm 34:8). The glory of His sweetness will be manifested during the millennial age and will be savored by His own throughout eternity.

"I have drunk my wine with my milk." What can this mean but the glory of His sufficiency? Wine stimulates,[1] milk strengthens. We need both; one without the other

---

[1]Using wine, here, in a symbolic rather than in a literal sense.

would produce imbalance. The Lord Jesus can keep these two aspects of life in proper balance for us. He is "the wine" and "the milk," and He alone satisfies. He satisfies us down here and He will satisfy us in Heaven. The two aspects of life suggested by wine and milk is what will make the millennial reign of Christ so abundantly satisfying. Then, not just Canaan but the whole world will be "flowing with milk and honey." Then, too, the Lord Jesus will fulfill His pledge and drink wine in the kingdom of God (Matthew 26:29).

The shepherd speaks finally of *his great exaltation:* "Eat, O friends; drink, yea, drink abundantly, O beloved." The marital bliss is shared only by the bridegroom and the bride, but beyond that there is something for their friends. Here we have another millennial concept. The joy and bliss of the marriage supper of the Lamb will be too good to be reserved for Heaven alone. It will spill over into this poor, wretched world. It will be shared by God's beleagured people, Israel. The great Shepherd-King will arise from the marriage supper and come back with His Bride to deal with the beast and the warring nations and to usher in that glorious millennial reign of His in which Israel will have her share.

VII. AN HOUR OF TESTIMONY

Song of Solomon 5:2 — 6:3

A. THE DREAM OF THE BELOVED (5:2-9)

1. A Dream of Excitement (5:2)

HOW PRACTICAL the lessons are which we glean from this book! The hour of tryst, in which we are occupied with the Word *of* God, gives way to the hour of testimony, when we are occupied with the word *for* God. Too often when "giving our testimony" we talk about ourselves and our experiences. A true testimony will be like that of the Shulamite— it will be occupied with *Him!*

Some of us rarely speak about the Lord, we are tongue-tied. We can speak eloquently enough, however, about themes which really interest us—a new motorbike, the baby, recipes, aches and pains. . . . The Shulamite was occupied with her beloved so she could talk naturally and eloquently about him. We shall be able to talk like that about the Lord Jesus only when our souls are full of Him.

The Shulamite relates a dream she had about herself and her beloved. Or was it a nightmare? She seems somewhat reluctant still, even in view of the shepherd's recent outpouring of his love for her. She dreamed of *a visitor who came* unexpectedly at night. "I sleep [or, I was asleep], but

my heart waketh: it is the voice of my beloved that knock-
eth, saying, Open to me, my sister, my love, my dove, my
undefiled: for my head is filled with dew" (5:2).

There are few things more discouraging than to arrive
when we should have been expected and find our knock
unanswered. How often has our great Lover come to the
door of our hearts only to find we are not expecting Him.
We are busy with other things—legitimate, essential perhaps, but things which crowd Him out of our minds.

The Shulamite dreams on of *a voice that called,* a voice
filled with passion: "Open to me, my sister, my love, my
dove, my undefiled."

There is also an accent of *propriety* about the call. An
unchaperoned visit would compromise his beloved's reputation. She is his "sister," a relationship of intimacy above
suspicion.

There is also an accent of *passion:* she is his "love." The
brother-sister relationship cannot be compared with the
husband-wife relationship. The shepherd does not give the
impression that he will settle for anything less than that,
but only when the proper time comes.

There is an accent of *prospect:* she is his "dove." The
shepherd speaks as though he expects her to come flying
to him. That is the prospect he has cherished.

There is an accent of *purity:* she is his "undefiled." Never
would he transgress in their pure and sacred relationship
though he calls with a voice of passion. It is not wild,
ungoverned passion, but passion with restraint. And so our
Beloved calls to us. His love never behaves unseemly, never
forces itself, never ravishes. It woos and waits.

The shepherd calls with *pathos:* "Open to me . . . for my
head is filled with dew, and my locks with the drops of the
night." He was drenched with dew. He longed to come in

out of the cold darkness into the warmth and shelter and light of his beloved's home.

How our Beloved longs for us to find a place for Him! It is nighttime now, the daystar has not yet risen. Every·thing is dark down here and all the powers of darkness are against Him. Doors and hearts are bolted and barred. Yet surely, in the Church, in the home of His Beloved, surely He should find a warm welcome and a ready response! Sad to say that is not always so. Sometimes the Church is as cold and indifferent as the world.

2. A Dream of Excuses (5:3-4)

The Shulamite never bothered to open the door and let him in. She simply allowed him to stand there, outside the bolted door, in the wet and cold of the night. She confesses *her silly reasons:* "I have put off my coat; how shall I put it on? I have washed my feet; how shall I defile them?" These are the very excuses the Church has made, through the ages, for refusing to give the Lord Jesus total access to its affairs and control over its activities.

The Church has consistently made *the relaxation excuse:* "I have done my share, I have had a busy day, I'm too tired. Let somebody else do it."

The Church has also been quick with *the ritual excuse:* "I have washed my feet; how shall I defile them?" In fact, for many the substitution of ritual for reality has long been a way of life. Many of America's churches are crowded on Sunday mornings with people who are making the ritual excuse without even realizing it. Even in fellowships where any formalism is suspect, ritualism creeps in. Some who would not think of missing the Lord's table make that observance the sum total of their commitment to the local church. They can sit back and relax, they have "washed their feet," so to speak.

The ritual excuse, however, can be even more subtle. There is always the trap of being so exhausted, so busy, even in the Lord's service, that we have no time for Him. Thus our daily quiet time either becomes neglected altogether or else it becomes perfunctory and sterile, a mere form. The Lord comes and knocks and calls but we do not take the time to let Him in.

The Shulamite had *a sad reward:* "My beloved put in his hand by the hole of the door." "My beloved thrust in his hand at the window" (Rotherham). The Companion Bible margin suggests the reading, "Then my beloved withdrew his hand" and comments that the Hebrew could literally be rendered "sent his hand away."

It would seem that the shepherd was about to force his way in, then changed his mind and went quietly away. Our Beloved will never force Himself upon us. If we will not open to Him when He comes He will leave us to ourselves. And we, like Joseph and Mary who spent a whole day without Jesus then spent the next three days in frantic search for Him, often do the same. We are so dull that we can sometimes go a week, a month, a year, half a lifetime "supposing Him to be in the company," when, as far as active fellowship is concerned, He withdrew long ago.

The Shulamite had *swift remorse:* "My beloved put in his hand by the hole of the door, and my bowels were moved for him." "And my feelings were deeply moved for him" (Rotherham).

Suddenly it dawned upon the Shulamite what she had done. She was covered with shame. Thank God for such a swift and sensitive response to the sudden loss of fellowship! She had raised a barrier, however, and that was not easily torn down. Many a couple has experienced this kind of situation. One makes a loving advance which is ignored or repulsed, resulting in a swift change of atmosphere. Belated apologies, explanations follow, but scars are not easily healed.

3. A Dream of Exercise (5:5-7)

The Shulamite is aroused now, deeply exercised as to what she should do. The beloved has gone! It would have been so easy to open the door to him when he first knocked. Now he has to be sought at great cost to herself.

The theme here is not salvation but fellowship. Nothing could alter her beloved's feelings toward her, but her feelings toward him need to be quickened. This may help explain those strange times in our own spiritual experience when we seem to find Heaven silent, prayer a drudgery. It is then the Lord would have us deepen our exercise and seek Him with all our heart.

What she decided: "I rose up to open to my beloved; and my hands dropped with myrrh, and my fingers with sweet smelling myrrh, upon the handles of the lock" (5:5). The Shulamite, with the quick instinct of love, plunged her hands into the ointment and ran to the door with her fingers still dripping with the fragrance. She would open the door! He would smell the perfume! It would tell him what she really felt. *What she discovered:* that she was too late: "I opened to my beloved; but my beloved had withdrawn himself, and was gone: my soul failed when he spake: I sought him, but could not find him; I called him but he gave me no answer" (5:6).

Fellowship with our Beloved is very delicately balanced. We can easily lose that sweet sense of oneness with

Himself, that happy spirit of intimacy. Deliberate, unconfessed sin, neglect of daily quiet time, disobedience to His
revealed will can do it. A sense of the Lord's presence is
something we must cultivate at all costs. We know from
our ordinary relationships that fellowship—a sense of mutual understanding, love, trust, and oneness—has to be
carefully cultivated. It does not just happen.

The Shulamite experienced *disappointment:* "My beloved
. . . was gone"; *dismay:* "My soul failed"; and *desperation:* "I
sought him, but I could not find him; I called him, but he
gave me no answer." We can picture her running around
the garden, peering into corners, calling his name and
finding nothing. We can see her standing by the gate
looking hopelessly up and down the deserted street, seeing
nothing but darkness and hearing nothing but the occasional cry of an owl or the call of the watchmen.

What she dared: to run out unprotected onto the streets
at night in a desperate effort to find her lost beloved. It was
a foolish thing to do. The Lord does not expect us to resort
to silly expedients to try to regain our lost fellowship.

As a result, *she was injured:* "The watchmen that went
about the city found me, they smote me, they wounded
me." Then *she was insulted:* "The keepers of the walls took
away my veil from me." Her character, her testimony,
even her virtue was imperiled by her foolish behavior.

There is no knowing to what lengths we will go, even
with the best of intentions, once we are out of fellowship
with the Lord. A believer out of touch with the Lord is like
a sheep astray from the shepherd, a prey to the hostile
influences that stalk the night.

The Shulamite awoke to find this only a dream. The
memory of it, however, lingered and its forceful, painful
lesson made a lasting impression on her heart.

4. A Dream of Exhortation (5:8-9)

The Shulamite turned to the court women with an urgent plea. We note *the message she relayed:* "I charge you, O daughters of Jerusalem, if ye find my beloved, that ye tell him, that I am sick of love" (5:8). How could she hope that these worldly women, who knew not her beloved, could convey her heart's cry to him?

Note also *the mockery she received:* "What is thy beloved more than another beloved, O thou fairest among women? what is thy beloved more than another beloved, that thou dost so charge us?" (5:9) What indeed! If they do not know him of course they could not appreciate him or understand such love as filled the soul of the Shulamite.

Nor can the world understand or appreciate our love for the Lord Jesus. Their shallow loves mean more to them. The world will come to our services at times. They will listen to us as we sing our hymns and gaze in astonishment at some of the words—"What can wash away my sin? Nothing but the blood of Jesus," for instance. They will listen to the preaching of the Word, then hurry out, still unsaved.

We say, "I can't understand why they don't get saved." We should understand—they don't know Him! Until they do, until the Holy Spirit reveals our Beloved to them, they will go on preferring what is offered to them by the prince of this world. They will not desire what is offered by the Lord Jesus, that great Shepherd of the sheep.

B. THE DESCRIPTION OF THE BELOVED (5:10-16)

Some years ago I was driving through a particularly beautiful part of Tennessee with an English evangelist.

Suddenly this friend, overcome by the glorious beauty of the scenery, burst out in a loud voice, with an expressive gesture of his hands, "Well done, Lord!"

Some such emotion stirs the soul of the Shulamite at the thought of her beloved. She was cut off from him, and the enemy was doing everything he could to cause her to succumb to his temptations. Her heart, however, was with her beloved and her soul cried out for him. Does our Beloved seem far away? Does the world seem terribly near? Are we battling fierce temptation or facing persistent opposition? Are our hearts in danger of growing cold? Then let us address our affections to the Lord Jesus as the Shulamite addressed hers to her absent love.

The Shulamite's thoughts revolve around *her beloved's purity:* "My beloved is white and ruddy" (5:10a). White is the symbol of purity, of holiness; ruddy, the symbol of glowing health.

The Lord Jesus was "white and ruddy," purity and passion were held in perfect balance in His life. He attracted men, won the sanctified adoration of women, drew little children irresistibly to Himself. All sin, all suggestiveness, all temptation simply withered and died in His presence. It was not that He was never tempted. It was, rather, that temptation stood no chance with Him. His purity causes the shining seraphim (those sinless sons of light whose personal holiness is such that they can stand in the immediate presence of God) to hide their faces in their wings before Him (Isaiah 6:2).

She mentions *her beloved's position:* "My beloved is . . . the chiefest among ten thousand" (5:10b). Our Beloved is much more than that! We see, in the Apostle John's vision, the throne of God, high and lifted up, with God Himself seated there, surrounded by the full circle of rainbow of emerald and ringed by Heaven's admiring throng. We see One step into the spotlight of glory, purer than the crystal stream that flows from the throne of God. It is the Lion of the tribe of Judah, the Root of David, the Lamb of Calvary. As He takes the scroll, the title deed of the planet Earth, from Him who sits upon the throne the heavenly hosts burst into song. There are ten thousand times ten thousand and Jesus is the chiefest of them all!

The Shulamite is taken up with *her beloved's person,* describing everything about him.

His sovereignty: "His head is as the most fine gold" (5:11a). Gold often symbolizes sovereignty in Scripture. In Nebuchadnezzar's dream of world dominion he saw an image of various metals, each one deteriorating in value as the eye progressed downward from the head of gold to the feet of clay. "Thou art this head of gold," Daniel told him (Daniel 2:38). It was an acknowledgment that God had bestowed upon this Gentile conqueror the right and the ability to subdue and rule the whole world.

The first thing that rivets our gaze as we look at the Beloved is His kingly majesty. Matthew saw it and wrote his Gospel to emphasize it. Our Lord put aside the splendor that was His before the worlds began when He entered into human life as a man among men. He was born of royal stock, of David's line; even though outwardly seeming to be but a Galilean peasant, raised as a laboring man to work at a carpenter's bench. Royal dignity clung to Him as a kingly robe. The demons acknowledged it. Peter saw it: "Thou art the Christ! Thou art the Lord's anointed." The hosts of Heaven acknowledge it.

> Sinners in derision crowned Him,
>   Mocking thus the Saviour's claim:

Saints and angels crowd around Him
Own His title, praise His name.
THOMAS KELLY

The kingship over the planet, which was invested for a fleeting moment in time in Nebuchadnezzar, over which would-be world conquerors have squabbled and fought since the days of Nimrod, which will be seized and held for 1,260 days or so by the devil's messiah, that kingship is Christ's!

Jesus shall reign where'er the sun
Doth his successive journeys run;
His kingdom stretch from shore to shore
'Til moons shall wax and wane no more.
ISAAC WATTS

His strength: "His locks are bushy, and black as a raven" (5:11b). Bushy black hair symbolizes virility. It suggests a person in the prime of life, just as gray hair would suggest one worn out with the years. The secret of Samson's great strength lay in his Nazarite locks. Samson, shorn of his locks, was as weak as a kitten, but Samson with that hair tumbling down to his shoulders could rend a lion. Samson, in the power of his strength, could pick up the gates of Gaza and carry them, bolts and bars and all, to the heights above the town.

It was thus with our Lord. He was strong, so very strong. Men could nail Him to a tree, but that was only because He allowed it. They could lock Him in a tomb and put Caesar's seal upon it, but when the prophesied three days and three nights were over, He arose, heaved the gates of hell upon His massive shoulders, and burst forth from the domain of death in mighty triumph.

Vainly they watch His bed, Jesus my Saviour!
Vainly they seal the dead, Jesus my Lord!
Up from the grave He arose,
With a mighty triumph o'er His foes;
He arose a Victor from the dark domain,
And He lives forever with His saints to reign:
He arose! He arose!
Hallelujah! Christ arose!

ROBERT LOWRY

His sight: "His eyes are as the eyes of doves by the rivers of waters, washed with milk, and fitly set" (5:12). "His eyes, like doves by the channels of water, bathed in milk, set as gems in a ring" (Rotherham).

What eyes our Beloved has! They gazed out over nothingness before the worlds began, and watched an expanding universe throw its tangle of stars over the limitless bounds of infinite space. Those eyes watched daylight banish darkness, the mountains heave themselves up from the seas, the waters above gaze down on the waters below. They watched verdure spread its carpet of green over valley and hill, life in a billion forms swarm through the seas and over the land to conquer the globe. They watched the dust of the earth come together to form a man. And, as He bent down to breathe life into that human clay, so Adam opened his eyes to look right into the eyes of Heaven's Beloved.

Those eyes of His read the soul of Judas, saw the blood money in his purse, hidden away beneath the folds of his robe, read the wretched traitor's eternal doom. Those eyes of His turned and looked on Peter so that Peter, filled with agony of soul, filled with bitter remorse, went out to his Gethsemane. Those eyes of His glowed with fellowship on the resurrection day, in that upper room, over a piece of broiled fish and honeycomb. Those eyes gaze now from glory to see us, wherever we are, the joy of His heart. These are the eyes which will gaze into ours when we see Him face to face.

His sweetness: "His cheeks are as a bed of spices, raised beds of sweet plants" (5:13a Darby). To be near him is to breathe the fragrance of balsam and spices, such sweetness as takes the breath away.

Shall we ever forget those cheeks of our Beloved? In the house of Caiaphas some great brute took His beard in calloused hands and literally wrenched it from His cheeks. And He allowed him to do it! Afterward, we can have little doubt, this deed of shame was forever forgiven. Such is the sweetness of our Beloved.

His sayings: "His lips like lilies, dropping sweet smelling myrrh" (5:13b). The most wonderful words that ever were uttered in the language of men fell from the lips of Jesus. Even His foes testified, "Never man spake like this man."

His skill: "His hands are as gold rings set with the beryl" (5:14a). Think of the hands of Jesus, the hands He placed on the heads of little children, the hands that touched the casket of the widow's son so that the dead man leaped to life, the hands He placed so warmly upon the leper. What hands He has! Royal hands, decked with beryl and fine gold; capable hands!

> Those loving hands that did such good,
> They nailed them to a cross of wood.
> ANN GILBERT

But now they hold the scepter and the fate of the planet lies in those nail-scarred, almighty hands.

His substance: "His belly [his body] is as bright [or polished] ivory overlaid with sapphires" (5:14b). The ivory typifies the body which Jesus took—a true, solid, material body, something which can be touched.

Before He entered into human life at Bethlehem, the Lord Jesus existed as the eternal, uncreated, self-existent Son of God, the second Person of the Godhead. He never ceased to be God, but when He was clothed with humanity He took upon Himself substance. He who had been from everlasting to everlasting a shining, immaterial, invisible spirit took upon Himself the substance of flesh and blood. He became a true man with a human body.

The ivory was bright, polished, brought to a beautiful finish. The inherent beauties of a substance are enhanced when it is polished, its sometimes hidden beauties become obvious to the eye. The Lord Jesus kept His body in perfect condition and control, always in subjection, the vehicle of the spirit within, the magnificent instrument through which could be expressed, in human terms, the life of God which was essentially His.

The ivory was overlaid with sapphires. The sapphire is a blue gem, a precious stone which displays the nature, color, and glory of Heaven. The body of Jesus was *of* Heaven (it was conceived by the Holy Ghost) and it is now *in* Heaven, forever glorified. He wears the same body He so wonderfully graced on earth, but it is now a resurrection body.

His stand: "His legs are as pillars of marble, set upon sockets of fine gold" (5:15a). Pillars of marble are the picture of stability and strength, sockets of gold another reference to sovereignty.

Think of the stand our Lord always took down here, first at the age of twelve: "Wist ye not that I must be about My Father's business?" (Luke 2:49) He took that stand again at the river Jordan; when Satan came to tempt Him; when He cleansed the Temple of the money-changers and merchants; when He attacked Satan's power structure in the hearts and minds and souls of men. He took that stand before Caiaphas, before Herod, and before Pilate. His legs were as pillars of marble.

Men were permitted to nail Him to the tree; the soldiers came, and broke the legs of the two thieves. His legs they dared not break, for the ancient prophecy had to be fulfilled—no bone of His was to be broken. His legs were as pillars of marble!

His splendor: "His countenance is as Lebanon, excellent as the cedars" (5:15b).

The face of the Lord Jesus was stamped with sublime glory. Never once did His face register doubt or perplexity or impatience. That countenance of His will one day banish both heaven and earth into oblivion (Revelation 20:11). That face will beam upon us when He welcomes us home.

> Oh, the soul-thrilling rapture when I view
> His blessed face,
> And the luster of His kindly beaming eye;
> How my full heart will praise Him for the mercy,
> love, and grace
> That prepared for me a mansion in the sky.
> FANNY J. CROSBY

His smile: "His mouth is most sweet" (5:16a). This wonderful Lord of ours is no remote, unapproachable, distant King. He is close to us, He loves us, His face will break into a ready smile the moment He sees us. We remember how this song begins. The Shulamite rhapsodies, "Let him kiss me with the kisses of his mouth!" No wonder she sums up this tenfold description of her beloved with the words, "Yea, he is altogether lovely. This is my beloved, and this is my friend."

C. THE DEPARTURE OF THE BELOVED (6:1-3)

The beloved's absence is the fact which gives the whole song so much pathos and power, so much drama and suspense.

1. The Response of Those Who Listened to the Shulamite (6:1)

The daughters of Jerusalem are astonished at this outpouring of love. Note *the question they put:* "Whither is thy beloved gone, O thou fairest among women?" (6:1a)

Her testimony has evoked a good response, it would seem. They want to know where to find her shepherd. That, after all, is the whole point and purpose of a testimony. We wish to present Christ to those who are held in the bonds of this world's prince, so that they will ask how they can find our Shepherd for themselves. We are reminded of the very first question in the New Testament. The wise men from the east came into Jerusalem asking, "Where is He that is born king of the Jews?" Our witness and testimony cause others to ask us to tell them how to find our Beloved.

Note *the quest they proposed:* to the Shulamite: "Whither is thy beloved turned aside? that we may seek with thee" (6:1b). Was this question sincere? Sometimes we have given our testimony about Christ and some seem to be impressed. They propose to accompany us to the place where, hopefully, He might be found. They even stir themselves and come with us to church, they read the books we give them, listen to sermons, ask meaningful questions. They seem to be sincere.

2. The Response of the One Who Listened to the Shepherd (6:2-3)

The Shulamite realized, of a sudden, she was "casting her pearls before swine"—to use our Lord's expressive phrase (Matthew 7:6). They were really not interested in her beloved at all, or, if they were, their motives were not sincere. It would do no good to tell them more, so she gave them a deliberately vague and evasive answer: "My beloved is gone down into his garden, to the beds of spices, to feed in the gardens, and to gather lilies" (6:2). In other words, she seems to say, "My beloved is in his own rightful place. He is where he belongs. He is doing those things which are a delight to his heart. He is engaged in a most beautiful occupation. He is busy feeding his flock and *I know where he is.* I know how to find him."

And so do we! We know where our Beloved is. He is in the garden of God, at God's right hand, and He is there as the great Shepherd of the sheep. He is leading His sheep beside still waters and into green pastures, He is doing all that is beautiful and blessed. It is not much use sharing that with the world, for what does the world know or care about the priesthood of the Lord Jesus Christ?

She says, "I know whose he is." "I am my beloved's, and my beloved is mine: he feedeth among the lilies" (6:3). She says in effect, "I am not going to tell you where he is but I'll tell you this much—He is mine. Go and seek him for yourselves, but remember, I am his and he is mine."

This time of testimony ends on rather a sad note, with

a realization that not all those who profess to want to know our Beloved are really sincere. We need to have a spirit of discernment. At least we can give our testimony, we can paint our Beloved in all the glory and beauty that is His, we can add: "I am His and He is mine." Such a relationship is possible for anyone. He says, "Ye shall seek Me, and find Me, when ye shall search for Me with all your heart" (Jeremiah 29:13).

VIII. AN HOUR OF TESTING

Song of Solomon 6:4—8:4

A. SOLOMON'S FLATTERIES (6:4—7:9)

NOW COMES THE FIERCEST TIME of testing. Solomon, evidently moved to jealousy of the shepherd who has won the heart of the woman he himself covets, suddenly appears and begins actively to court the Shulamite with flattery.

1. Solomon's Flatteries Resound (6:4-10)

You are fair (6:4-7). Solomon thinks first of *that which is imperial:* "Thou art beautiful, O my love, as Tirzah, comely as Jerusalem, terrible as an army with banners" (6:4). This country girl, with none of the airs and graces of the harem beauties, outdid them all in stately grace, simplicity, and natural dignity.

Tirzah later became the royal residence of the kings of Israel, after the division of the kingdom and until Omri built Samaria. It was situated in a beautiful part of the country. The very name Tirzah means "delightful." Jerusalem was the city of the great King, the city of God, where, of all places on this planet, God has been pleased to place His name. It was there that the Temple was being built, where worship was to be centered. And what bolder or braver sight could be suggested than an army with banners? In other words, the Shulamite has vanquished, devastated, conquered Solomon!

Solomon is not allowed to take her by force, even with all the power that a king could command. Like Satan, in the garden of Eden, he must rather persuade her to allow him to triumph over her.

In much the same way Satan knows he does not stand a chance against the Church. Jesus himself said so: "The gates of hell shall not prevail against it" (Matthew 16:18). The gate, in an oriental city, was the seat of government, where the laws were framed, decisions made, and business transacted. Nothing can prevail against the Church as long as she stays true to Christ. To the hosts of hell she is, indeed, "terrible as an army with banners."

Solomon realizes *that which is impossible:* "Turn away thine eyes from me, for they have overcome me" (6:5a). He cannot stand the gaze of the Shulamite. She can see right through him, and he knows he has no chance at all.

If only the Church would remember that, and take a good, hard look at the seducer of our souls. Yes, "star of the morning," "prince of the power of the air," "god of this world"—there he is, the serpent, the devil, Satan, deceiver, murderer, liar, the lawless one, the spirit who works in the children of disobedience. Look at him with an eye trained in truth by the Word of God. He cannot stand that.

Solomon thinks of *that which is impeccable:* "Thy hair is as a flock of goats on the slopes of Gilead. Thy teeth are like a flock of sheep which go up from the washing; which have all borne twins, and none is barren among them. As a piece of pomegranate are thy temples" (6:5b-7 Darby).

This is the very language of the shepherd (see 4:1-3).

Solomon now employs the same words himself. That is exactly the way the tempter operates. He quotes Scripture. He did it to the Lord of glory Himself in the wilderness temptation. He does it in every false cult that he spawns in Christendom. He is a master at picking up the words of the great Shepherd Himself and using those very words to deceive and to destroy.

The Bible teaches that a woman's hair is her glory. Solomon recognized the *glory* of the Shulamite, her *gladness,* (the mention of her white teeth suggests her ready smile), and her *goodness* (suggested by her temples being like a pomegranate—blushing red). It is the same with the Church in this world. Its glory is displayed in such a way as to bring honor to its Head (1 Corinthians 11:1-16). It derives its joy and gladness from sources other than those in the world. Its goodness is of a caliber that cannot be found in the unregenerate sons of men.

Think of what a dreadful place this world was, and still is, apart from the true Church. It is only where the Church has gone and the gospel has been preached that people have, in any measure, been liberated from bondage, brutality, beastiality, and wretchedness. It is the Church which first built hospitals, orphanages, schools, asylums, leper colonies, and rescue homes. In any measure in which the world does these things today it reveals the extent to which its conscience has been pricked by the Church. The world pays lips service, at times, to the true Church, which it cannot help but admire. Yet it rejoices most when she falls.

You Are First (6:8-10). "There are threescore queens, and fourscore concubines, and virgins [damsels] without number." The margin of the Companion Bible renders the phrase "there are threescore queens" as "I have threescore queens." Moffatt renders it "sixty queens had Solomon, eighty concubines, maidens without number."[1] But you, Solomon implies, can be the first. The great tempter of mankind has religions without number, some of them queenly and great, as the world looks at things. He would love to add the true Church to his collection. Indeed, he does have a harlot bride, the apostate church (Revelation 17), but he cannot seduce the true Church, the pure and holy bride of Christ. She is going to be the first some day—first in the universe, sharing the splendor and magnificence of her Shepherd-Lord. She is already seated with Him, spiritually, in heavenly places, far above principalities and powers, thrones and dominions. In the coming glory age she will be manifestly first throughout all of God's vast empires in space.

Not only did Solomon put the Shulamite first *by count* but also *by contrast:* "My dove, my undefiled, is but one; she is the only one of her mother, she is the choice one of her that bare her" (6:9a); *by confession:* "The daughters saw her, and blessed her; yea, the queens and the concubines, and they praised her" (6:9b); and *by conquest:* "Who is she that looketh forth as the morning, fair as the moon, clear as the sun, and terrible as an army with banners?" (6:10)

There are many religious systems in this world which are outwardly beautiful. But who can compare these

---

[1]This verse clinches the argument that Solomon cannot possibly be a type of Christ in this song. Christ had only one Bride. Those who still insist that he is evade the force of this verse by saying that Solomon was merely asserting, "There are sixty queens." But as various translators have shown, such a handling of the verse is evasive. What other queens and concubines would he be talking about if not his own? Once we see Solomon as the tempter the difficulty is resolved.

systems with the magnificence of the true Church? The Church stands alone. Christianity is unique. Christ is not to be compared with Buddha or Krishna or Confucius. Christ is incomparable, the eternal, uncreated, self-existing Son of God, over all, blessed forevermore. The true Church of Christ stands apart by count, by contrast, by confession, and by conquest.

As far as the world is concerned, as far as Satan is concerned, as far as all our foes are concerned, God has drawn the line in the sand. He says to those who tamper with His Church just what He says to the heaving billows and inrushing tides: "Hitherto shalt thou come, but no farther and here shall thy proud waves be stayed?" (Job 38:11)

Whenever the Church has arisen in all its pristine purity and might, the forces of hell have fallen back. Every now and then the Holy Spirit revives the Church, souls are saved in vast numbers, and the vile forces that sap away at human life are hurled back. Satan fears the Church. There have been times when he has unloosed violence against it, but he has always been the loser, for the blood of the martyrs has proven, again and again, to be the very seed of the Church.

Jesus said: "Upon this rock I will build My church; and the gates of hell shall not prevail against it" (Matthew 16:18). The Church, to the powers of the pit, is as terrible as an army with banners. Great and glorious is the Church when, like the Shulamite, it lays aside all worldly weapons and stands arrayed solely in its pristine purity and power. Satan cannot harm her then.

The time of testing for the Shulamite is by no means over. We have next her firm response to the pressure being brought to bear upon her by the king.

2. Solomon's Flatteries Rebuffed (6:11-13)

The Shulamite rejects Solomon's suggestions instantly. She is not interested. That, of course, is the very best way to deal with temptation. If we toy with it, flirt with it, give it a moment's thought as a possible option—then down we go.

That is what Eve did in Eden. She entertained the thought Satan put into her mind and thus showed she was prepared to discuss and debate it. When Satan saw Eve toying with a thought which was contrary to the known and revealed word of God he knew he had already won. Soon the doubt became an outright denial and the denial was replaced by a delusion. When we are tempted, the answer must be a firm and unequivocal "No!"

We note *the Shulamite's explanation:* "I went down into the garden of nuts to see the fruits of the valley, and to see whether the vine flourished, and the pomegranates budded. Or ever I was aware, my soul made me like the chariots of Ammi-nadib" (6:11-12). The critics have had difficulty with that last statement. J. N. Darby translates it: "Before I was aware, my soul set me upon the chariots of my willing people." Rotherham is even clearer: "I know not [how it was] my soul set for me the chariots of my willing people." The King James text renders the puzzling passage as a proper name—"the chariots of Ammi-nadib." The Hebrew Ammi-nadib can be rendered as "the chariots of my people," "the noble," or "my noble people."

The Shulamite is telling Solomon that she was attending to her own business, inspecting the orchards and the vineyards, when suddenly she found herself surrounded by the chariots of the country's nobility. She was innocent of any curiosity about the presence of the royal entourage in the country. She had been going about her normal affairs when suddenly she had been swept up by Solomon's people and her liberty had been taken away.

The trouble with playing with temptation is that we always get in deeper and deeper. As someone has said, we sow a thought and reap an action, sow an action and reap a habit, sow a habit and reap a character; sow a character and reap an eternal destiny. We make friends with the wrong crowd, for instance, or show an interest in some worldly pleasure which is harmful to spiritual life and before we know it we have become involved.

The Holy Spirit tells us we are to "flee youthful lusts." We are to avoid any compromising situation. If perchance we find ourselves involved in one which is not of our making, we are to make it quite clear that we are there by mistake and that we are not in the market for what is offered. We need to watch out for these "chariots of Amminadib," as they will pounce upon us if we are not careful, even when we are attending to our legitimate affairs.

Note *the seducer's exclamation:* "Return, return, O Shulamite; return, return, that we may look upon thee" (6:13a). It is generally believed that Shulem is the same as Shunem, a village just north of Jezreel and mentioned several times in the Old Testament. Solomon calls her "the Shulamite" (the first time this name is mentioned in the song), using a name which perhaps had already passed into the poetry of the land for "the fairest among women." What Abishag, David's wife in his old age, was in the annals of Hebrew history—the most beautiful woman in the world, the most desirable daughter of Jerusalem—that is what the shepherdess was to Solomon, or so he said.

Note, too, *the Shulamite's exasperation:* she asks, "What will ye see in the Shulamite?" (6:13b) Back comes the ready response of the suitor, "As it were the dance of two camps" (Darby). Solomon and his jaded court wanted the lovely shepherdess to put on a sensual show for them. Her obvious disinterest in the king provokes him now to sensuality and suggestiveness. The moment we effectively repulse temptation, and let those who are tempting us know that we are definitely not interested, the real, ugly nature of the tempter will be revealed.

3. Solomon's Flatteries Resumed (7:1-9)

Solomon's wisdom which was originally "from above" has become "earthly, sensual, devilish" (James 3:15) as the book of Ecclesiastes clearly shows. In his pursuit of popularity, pleasure, and power he has become a fool. Solomon had failed. The Shulamite, like Job in his hour of testing, sinned not nor answered foolishly. What a picture she is of the true Church of Christ.

Solomon's bold description of the Shulamite (7:1-5). He makes no mention of her inner beauties, of her courage and constancy, of her loyalty and purity. He is interested just in her body.

Her feet: "How beautiful are thy feet with shoes, O prince's daughter!" (7:1) Doubtless when the Shulamite was first abducted by the king she was dressed like any other peasant girl, her feet either bare or shod with simple sandals. Now she is made to stand before her captor in jeweled slippers. Solomon has placed her shoes on her feet.

Shoes were the first thing the father put on the prodigal when he returned from his wandering ways. When Moses stood before God at the burning bush, God told him to take his shoes off. In other words, there was no ground for familiarity between Moses and the One in that burning bush. Moses was to keep his distance; the prodigal was brought into the house, his feet shod as proof of acceptance and his right to draw near.

The Shulamite's shoes suggest her standing and her feet suggest her steps. Solomon begins his description at the point where the Shulamite came into contact with the world, and he found beauty there, beauty which he himself had placed there in his effort to win her to his world.

A good place for us to begin our consideration of the Church, her standing and steps, is where she makes contact with the world. Whenever we have to make contact with this present evil world our feet should be "shod with the preparation of the gospel of peace" (Ephesians 6:15), for "How beautiful are the feet of them that . . . bring glad tidings of good things" (Romans 10:15). We are in this world to make contact for Christ!

Solomon would have had the Shulamite stretch out those feet and admire the costly sandals he offered her. He would have had her rest her feet or else walk a path of luxury and ease. That is just what the tempter would like to persuade us to do—put our feet up. But that is not why we are here.

Then there were *her thighs:* "the joints of thy thighs are like jewels" (7:1b). In Scripture, the thigh is associated with strength. When Jacob wrestled with the angel he was able to maintain his own, in the carnal, natural strength that was his, until the mighty Wrestler reached out and touched the hollow of his thigh. The moment his thigh was put out of joint Jacob could no longer fight, he was a broken man, he could only cling! It was as a man with all his natural power judged and spent that he entered into spiritual power to walk henceforth as a prince with God. When our lovely Lord comes back to reign He will have His sword girded on His thigh—the symbol of power and strength.

We can see then the force of Solomon's remark. He wanted that which spoke of strength in the Shulamite to be made subservient to his pleasures. So Satan would like to take that which speaks of the strength of the Church and bring it down into the dust, or else array it in trappings of his own system and make it serve his own ends. He has succeeded very well along that line with the false church— we have only to think, for instance, how Rome has traded spiritual power for secular pomp. The "thighs" of the false church are adorned with costly vestments. She is arrayed in purple and gold and scarlet—but she is useless for God (Revelation 17:4).

Satan is adept at persuading us to trade our spiritual power for some piece of the world's tinsel—a ribbon, a title, a promotion. These are the gossamer threads he often uses to get us to use our strength for this world instead of for the world to come, for him instead of for our Beloved.

Solomon describes *the Shulamite's form:* "Thy navel is like a round goblet, which wanteth not liquor [spiced wine]: thy belly is like a heap of wheat set about with lilies. Thy two breasts are like young roes that are twins. Thy neck is as a tower of ivory" (7:2-4a). We are conscious here of Solomon's total disregard for the Shulamite's embarrassment. Behind his flatteries lies a reality of which Solomon was quite unaware—the incomparable beauty of the Church. Even as Caiaphas, in his bitter hatred, spoke true words of Christ, words that transcended his comprehension, so Solomon, in his carnality and desire, spoke true words of the Church which have an eternal significance far beyond anything he could have dreamed. This is why this song has found its place in the canon of Scripture. God, who knows how to make the wrath of man to praise Him, knows how to make the carnality of man to praise Him too. He takes here the words that Solomon uttered and endows them with significance, on a higher, purer, spiritual plane, such as Solomon never could have imagined.

The navel is the symbol of *independent life*. Once we were mysteriously wrapped in another's life and existence but, in due time, we were brought to birth and given a life of our own. Nothing but a vestigial token, a navel, now remains of that previous life mystery.

It is thus with the Church. It had a hidden life of mystery throughout the entire Old Testament period. Its mother was Israel, but through the Old Testament era it lay hidden and concealed in the nation's womb. It was brought to birth at Pentecost in that upper room in Jerusalem when the Holy Spirit came down and baptized those individual believers into the mystical body of Christ—the Church.

In the purposes of God, the umbilical cord was cut and the Church was given a new, vibrant, dynamic life of its own, never again to return to its former tie to Israel. This explains why we can see the Church in some of the typology in the Old Testament. We can see the Church in its hidden, embryonic form, hidden away in the womb of many an Old Testament Scripture. We can see it in the story of Joseph and Asenath, of Isaac and Rebekah, of Ruth and Boaz; in some of the types of the tabernacle; and in some of the mystical statements of the Psalms.

Solomon, of course, knew nothing of the Church, but the Holy Spirit did. That is why he records Solomon's words. There is something magnificent even in Solomon's clumsy reference to the Shulamite's navel being a "goblet of spiced wine," for that is what the Church is in the counsels of God—new wine. Jesus said that no man would put new wine into old wineskins—they would simply burst. The worn-out wineskin of Judaism had served its purpose by the time "the day of Pentecost was fully come," so a new vessel was prepared to receive the new wine of the Spirit of God.

The baptism of the Spirit is for the Church alone. It is spiced wine indeed, adding a tang to life, now and for eternity, unique in all of God's gracious dealings with the children of men. The baptism of the Spirit takes a believing person and makes that person a member of the mystical body of Christ, fit to share in the very life of God Him-self! This is something unique to the Church.

Solomon refers to the *incomparable loveliness* of the Shulamite: "Thy belly is like a heap of wheat set about with lilies" (7:2b). With a grasp of poetry we cannot help but admire, Solomon brings together the glory of the golden grain and the fragrance of the flowers of the field.

Wheat is the Holy Spirit's symbol for the Church. Israel, as a nation, is likened to the fig, the olive, the vine, even to the stately cedar. These are all trees, firmly rooted in the earth, fit symbols for God's earthly people. Wheat is quite different, reaped from the earth annually in successive harvests. It is left here—like the Church—only so long as is necessary for it to grow to maturity, lovely and useful, and then it is taken away from this world altogether.

Solomon continued: "Thy two breasts are like two young roes that are twins" (7:3). Solomon spoke of the Shulamite's womanly shape as a pair of fawns, twins of the roe deer, standing hidden in the long grass, far from the hunter's bow. She held herself aloof from him, as one whose *infinite love* was pledged to another.

We, as the people of God in this world of lust and licentiousness, will never appear more attractive, more desirable, more worth conquering than when we keep ourselves pure and our hopes and affections fixed on our

Beloved. The Lord desires above all else that the Church's innate capacity for life and love be reserved for Him. Only then can it become productive for God.

"Thy neck is as a tower of ivory" (7:4a). The Shulamite's *invincible loyalty* was not to be cowed or conquered. The neck of the Shulamite is the symbol here of unyieldedness to sin, of firmness of personal resolve not to bow to Solomon's desires.

Her Features (7:4b-5): "Thine eyes [are] like the fishpools in Heshbon, by the gate of Bath-rabbim" (7:4b). As he looked at the Shulamite, Solomon saw *something desirable*.

Heshbon was originally a Moabite town, conquered by Moses and converted into a Levitical city. Levitical cities were scattered up and down the promised land, set apart for the tribe of Levi, which had been consecrated to serve God. The Levites were to act as a sanctifying influence on the Hebrew people. Heshbon itself was about twenty miles east of the river Jordan, not far from where the river buries itself in the Dead Sea. The Dead Sea region is a wilderness, but Heshbon was situated at the site of an excellent spring which made it particularly desirable. A couple of pools stood at the gate of this city, a most attractive sight.

That is what the Church is to be in the world—an oasis in the desert, a life-giving pool of delight and refreshment in a barren wilderness destitute of all that feeds the spirit. The Church is to be something more desirable, a Levitical city, an enclave of God in a hostile world.

Something Defiant: "Thy nose is as the tower of Lebanon which looketh toward Damascus" (7:4c). Why did Solomon describe the Shulamite's nose in such a way? We can easily picture this patient young woman, sick and tired of Solomon's blandishments, as she tosses her head defiantly.

Thus the Church in the world has an air of defiance.

Surrounded by countless foes, it is the subject of endless allurements, besieged day and night by the tempter in his efforts to catch it off guard. The true Church turns up its nose at him! It despises him, has no use for him at all.

Something Distinguished: "Thine head upon thee is like Carmel" (7:5a). Mount Carmel is impressive as it lifts its magnificent head from the surrounding plains and from the shores of the Mediterranean Sea. It is distinguished, exalted, very high.

The Church often depreciates herself, yet she is a partaker of the divine nature. She is far more distinguished, in the order of things, than Michael the archangel or Gabriel the herald angel, than Lucifer (son of the morning, as he was in his unfallen state), the anointed cherub, highest of all created beings. Satan, archfiend of the pit, knows it well, which helps explain why he so very much desires to get his hands on her.

"The hair of thine head is like purple; the king is held in the galleries" (7:5b). Darby renders that last phrase, "the king is fettered by thy ringlets." Solomon saw *something disturbing*. He saw royalty in the Shulamite's hair, in the way it fell down upon her shoulders, shining like purple, like the splendid robes of a queen.

There is something disturbing to the tempter about the Church he would like to lay low. She has an imperial air about her, and he knows that he has been vanquished by her. That seat of imperial power, to which he himself aspired before the fall, is hers by sovereign right. The Church is already seated there in Christ, far above all principalities and powers and every name that is named. Satan is at once both repelled by the Church and yet drawn by her to his own destruction. He plays with the greatest and most culpable temptation of all, the temptation to seize and ravish the Church of God.

Solomon's burning desire for the Shulamite longs to see her in all her dignity and *to seize her in all her desirability:* "How fair and how pleasant art thou, O love, for delights! This thy stature is like to a palm tree, and thy breasts to clusters of grapes. I said, I will go up to the palm tree, I will take hold of the boughs thereof: now also thy breasts shall be as clusters of the vine, and the smell of thy nose like apples; And the roof of thy mouth like the best wine for my beloved, that goeth down sweetly, causing the lips of those that are asleep to speak" (7:6-9). Stately she is like a palm tree, superb she is, like the fully ripened fruit of the vine!

Solomon's *strength is asserted, his senses aroused.* "I will," he says, "I will, I will, I will!" He has made up his mind to seize her by force, careless of the consequences. He is like an intoxicated man who can no longer control what he says or does. Such too is Satan's desire to conquer the Church. That fact alone helps explain much of the history of the past two thousand years. Satan is the victim of his own fall, and of his own fierce lusts.

B. THE SHULAMITE'S FIDELITY (7:10—8:4)

What a glorious woman was this Shulamite! Nowhere does she appear lovelier than now as she quietly and quickly puts her tempter in his place, with such firmness and finesse that Solomon makes no further attempt to bend her to his will. Here we have the essence of successfully resisting temptation. What the Shulamite did, we must do. Indeed, it is exactly what the Lord Jesus did when tempted of Satan in the wilderness. When the evil one came to Him with those three temptations the Lord quietly answered him with the written Word. Subdued by the Lord's firmness and fidelity, the tempter crept away. So Solomon leaves the Shulamite alone from this point on. Never again will his voice be raised in this song.

1. The Shulamite's Assertion (7:10)

To all the eloquence of the tempter the Shulamite had but one reply: "I am my beloved's, and his desire is toward me." That was that! What better way to fight the tempter and his wiles?

She stated her position first *in terms of possession:* "I am not my own. I belong to another. You are asking me to give what is not mine to bestow. My life has been pledged to another." How sufficient! How strong! Solomon had no answer to that, nor does Satan. It is an unassailable position for us to take in the moment of temptation.

But how could a shepherd hold his own against such a giant as Solomon? To understand that we need to go back a few chapters to the historical narratives of the Old Testament, to David, that Old Testament shepherd. He is one of the great life-types of Christ, standing in direct line with Abel and Joseph and Moses.

It was as the anointed shepherd that David went forth to meet the foe, Goliath of Gath, who held such absolute sway over the valley of Elah. David made no attempt to meet him on his terms, arrayed in the clumsy armor of Saul, which he put aside as useless for this fight. Down into the valley David went, taking with him the symbol of his shepherd life, his bag. He was going to defeat Goliath not as a soldier, statesman, scholar, or swordsman, but as a shepherd.

David went deliberately into that valley to destroy one who had the power of death, and the battle was over in a flash. David first bruised the enemy's head then, using the foe's own weapon against him, left him a headless corpse on the side of the hill.

It was then that Jonathan gave his heart to David and, in giving him his heart, he gave him everything—his robe, his sword, his bow, his girdle, his throne, his crown. "Now I belong to David!" was the song of his soul.

Saul, who hated David and all that he stood for, noticed it first. It did not take Saul long to treat Jonathan's love for David as high treason: "Thou son of the perverse rebellious woman, do not I know that thou hast chosen the son of Jesse to thine own confusion?" (1 Samuel 20:30) The world can never understand loyalty to the shepherd. For a person to place fame and fortune, heart and life, body and soul at the feet of the shepherd is quite beyond the comprehension of those who do not love him.

We lift the whole story to higher ground and look away to David's greater Son. We see our Beloved, that true Shepherd of the sheep. We think of the day He went down into the valley of death for us. Our hearts go out to Him like the heart of Jonathan. Our soul is knit with the soul of the Saviour.

The Shulamite had given her heart to her shepherd the way the mighty men of David gave their hearts to their shepherd, the way we have given our hearts to our Shepherd. "I am my beloved's," she said. Solomon was helpless in the face of such loyalty and love.

Our tempter is helpless when we take this same stand. He is no match for the Shepherd. The Shulamite was on solid ground when she stated her position to Solomon in terms of possession. The outward advantages seemed to be with Solomon, but the real power was with the shepherd.

The Shulamite also spoke *in terms of passion:* "I am my

beloved's, and his desire is toward me" (7:10b). That was the position Solomon had been trying to undermine, but she put the relationship on more unassailable ground: "*His* desire is toward me.*" What a wonderful way to combat temptation. All we need to say to the tempter is, "There's my Beloved, there's my Shepherd, go and take up the matter with Him, for His desire is toward me."

Once, Satan did take on that Shepherd. It was after our Lord entered into human life, clothed Himself with humanity, and agreed to meet Satan on those terms. Satan attacked Him in His weakness in the wilderness only to flee stabbed through by the sword of the Spirit.

Satan took Him on again at Calvary. He thought he had vanquished Him then. But Calvary was all part of the divine plan, the cross the chosen instrument by which Christ was to enter into death, descend into the world of the dead to proclaim His triumph there, and then to emerge triumphant indeed. He lives now in the power of an endless life, He has carried the marks of Calvary up to glory, and now He sits enthroned at the right hand of God.

"His desire is toward me." Just think of it: "*His* desire is toward *me!*" Think for a moment of who He really is, the eternal, uncreated, self-existing second Person of the Godhead, creator of every star in space. There is not an angel or an archangel, not a cherub or a seraph, not one among all the principalities and powers, thrones and dominions in the spirit world that does not bow the knee to Him. He is omnipotent, omniscient, and omnipresent, possessing all the attributes and prerogatives of Deity. Does He need praise? Ten thousand times ten thousand voices in the celestial choir awake to the echoes of the everlasting hills to proclaim His praise. Does He need service? A million million exalted spirits hang upon His words and rush to do His bidding. Does He need love? The sinless sons of light in yonder bright regions of joy fall in adoration at His feet. Yet *His* desire is toward *me!* That should put any temptation from the seducer into its proper perspective. In the face of such monumental truth temptation loses all its power.

2. The Shulamite's Aspiration (7:11—8:3)

Now that her thoughts are finally freed from Solomon's flatteries and are again fixed on her beloved, the longings of the Shulamite's heart are able to find full expression. She recounts *what she wanted* (7:11-13)—first of all *to be with her beloved:* "Come, my beloved" (7:11a). Is that not always the cry of a loving heart separated from the object of its affection?

The thought of the Lord's coming is intended to be just such an antidote to the attractions and allurements of this present evil age. "And every man that hath this hope in him purifieth himself" (1 John 3:3). Let us once get the thought of the Lord's coming firmly fixed in our hearts and minds, and it will garrison us against temptation. His coming may be today!

The Shulamite not only wanted to be with her beloved, she wanted *to flee with her beloved:* "Let us go forth into the field; let us lodge in the villages. Let us get up early to the vineyards; let us see if the vine flourish, whether the tender grape appear, and the pomegranates bud forth: there will I give thee my loves. The mandrakes give a smell, and at our gates are all manner of pleasant fruits, new and old, which I have laid up for thee, O my beloved" (7:11b-13).

She had somewhere to go with him—into the field, the villages, the vineyard. In other words, she wanted to go to the places where she had labored so diligently in times past, before she had been waylaid by Solomon.

Have we lived to such purpose that a similar desire could be the earnest expression of our hearts? Would we like to be able to take our Beloved with us to the scenes of past labors? How thrilling it would be to be able to say to Him, "Here, Lord, in this community I was known by everyone as a Christian. Here I sowed the seed of the gospel. Here, Lord, in this corner of the vineyard I was faithful. Here I invested my time and talents for You. Here I gave prodigally of my means. Here I sought to lay up treasure in Heaven."

The Shulamite had *something to give to him*—of all she might have offered him surely what he would have wanted most—*the fervor of her love* ("There will I give you my endearments" is another rendering), and *the fruit of her life*. Mandrakes were love-apples often associated in the East with physical love. In anticipation of her wedding day the Shulamite had been storing up things new and old for her beloved. She had loved him for a long time, and her love had been fruitful.

Our Beloved wants no more than that. What can we give Him, this omnipresent, omniscient One? He has everything that Deity could command or create. But there are two things we can give Him which He will prize: the fervor of our love and the fruit of our life.

The Shulamite *recounts what she wished:* that the period of waiting were over so she could *shout her love for her beloved publicly without being despised:* "O that thou wert as my brother, that sucked the breasts of my mother! when I should find thee without, I would kiss thee; yea, I should not be despised" (8:1). We must remember that the setting of this song was an oriental one. Strict social conventions kept a bride and prospective groom apart. It would have been highly improper for her, under the rigid social code of the day, to have expressed her love for him in a public and open way, but it would not have been improper for her to embrace her brother. The Shulamite wished she could be more open and forcible in expressing all her heart felt for her beloved.

How often we wish the same! We are living in a world where social customs and conventions can be strong. In our culture, it is quite accepted for a person to go to a football game and yell, shout, and cheer, to wave his arms and throw his hat in the air. It is quite out of place to get excited about the Lord. The moment a person expresses any religious emotion he is called a fanatic. A few unconventional souls go ahead and shout anyway! Most of us wish that we had their courage or, at least, that frowning social inhibitions were not so strong.

The Shulamite longed *to share her love for her beloved privately without being disgraced:* "I would lead thee, and bring thee into my mother's house, who would instruct me: I would cause thee to drink of spiced wine of the juice of my pomegranate" (8:2). For her to take a man home, even to her mother's house, and give him spiced wine and inflame his passions, would have been an unthinkable liberty.

She wished she could *show her love for her beloved passionately without being defiled:* "His left hand should be under my head, and his right hand should embrace me" (8:3). Oh, that she were already married, that the wedding day had come! She is looking beyond the present to the future when all restraints would be forever and properly removed.

This is the height of love for Christ. Have we ever felt like the Shulamite? Have there been times when our longing for the Lord has welled up in inexpressible longing and desire? Have we ever felt like trampling on every social restraint and shouting aloud: "My Jesus, I love you!" Has the longing for the consummation of things in glory become overwhelming?

3. The Shulamite's Asperity (8:4)

Solomon apparently gets the court women to intercede for him once more. They tried twice before and failed (2:7; 3:5) but now they try again.

The Shulamite turns on them with asperity and repudiates them: "I charge you, O daughters of Jerusalem, that ye stir not up, nor awake my love, until he [she] please." She says, "Don't incite my love, don't excite my passions." (The words "until he" are in the feminine to agree with the gender of the Hebrew word for love). Thus for the third time the Shulamite tells Solomon's women to leave her alone and to stop seeking to divert her love from her beloved to theirs. It is the final statement in this long section of the song.

We are up against a persistent tempter. He never gives up. He might assume a low profile, but his agents are there working for him. Any genuine expression of love from our hearts for Christ will certainly be followed by a fresh attempt by the tempter to capitalize on our moods in order to bring about a fall. No wonder we need to be on our guard. There is nothing holy to Satan, not even our love for the Lord Jesus. He would like to tamper with that most of all.

IX. AN HOUR OF TRIUMPH

Song of Solomon 8:5-14

A. THE SHULAMITE AND HER BELOVED (8:5-7)

IT IS ALMOST TIME to bring the story to a close and like most good stories it has a happy ending. True, life is often enough grim and unhappy and storytellers sometimes end their tales thus for that reason. But the song ends on a high note with the Shulamite and her shepherd living happily together and with the tempter thwarted.

The closing paragraphs of the song deal with that time of triumph with which the romance ends.

1. They Come Together (8:5a)

The first voice to be heard is that of the companions of the shepherd, friends of the bridegroom: "Who is this that cometh up from the wilderness, leaning up on her beloved?" (8:5a)

We are not told when it takes place or how the shepherd secures the release of his bride from the prison in which she lay, surrounded by guards and women of the court of the frustrated worldly prince. All we know is that the miracle took place. The shepherd has come, she is with her beloved at last. He and his friends join in the joy and rejoicing of the coming together of the bride and the groom.

That is the way it is to be with us. We are on tiptoe with expectancy for Jesus is coming again. Although we know not when, we know for sure that one of these days He will cleave the clouds, "descend from heaven with a shout, with the voice of the archangel, and with the trump of God: and the dead in Christ shall rise first: Then we which are alive and remain shall be caught up" (1 Thessalonians 4:15-16). We shall be carried bodily from this present evil world. The forces which hold us earthbound will be dissolved and we shall be changed. In a moment, in the twinkling of an eye, corruption will be changed into incorruption, mortality into immortality. Death will be swallowed up in victory.

2. They Commune Together (8:5b-7)

We can imagine that after such a traumatic separation the shepherd and the Shulamite had a great deal to say to each other. Note *what they remembered:* "I raised thee up under the apple tree: there thy mother brought thee forth; there she brought thee forth that bare thee" (8:5b). He is recalling the time and place where life and love had their birth.

It is something for us to remember too, the place where we first met our great Shepherd, when we were born into the family of God, when life began. There are some who cannot remember the exact moment of their new birth. But He remembers when and where He was first able to kindle in our hearts love for Himself and life forevermore.

Note *what they relished.* First was *love's seal:* "Set me as a seal upon thine heart, as a seal upon thine arm" (8:6a), or as it may be rendered, "Wear me as a seal close to your heart, wear me like a ring upon your hand." The hand and the heart are thus linked together. The seal is the signet ring which in olden days was regarded as the actual signature of the owner, representing the person who wore it. These signatures, or seals, were used to make contracts binding, a symbol of ownership.

We still use rings similarly today. When a young man and woman fall in love and they plan a future together, he presents her with an engagement ring. She wears it as a token of their intention to marry, a sign that her affections are completely engaged. She has given her hand to her beloved and upon that hand she wears the seal, the signet, the symbol of love.

The Lord Jesus has told us of His great love for us, a love that passes knowledge, a love which is the most astonishing fact in the universe. He wants to protect and provide for us, to be near and dear to us. He wants us to be His, to share His home, to reign with Him. And, as the evident token of His great, magnificent love, He has given us an "engagement ring," the earnest of our inheritance, the priceless token of the reality of His love: He has given us the Holy Spirit. Paul actually calls the Holy Spirit "the earnest" (Ephesians 1:14). The Holy Spirit is His seal, His signet, the symbol of His love. We are pledged now to watch and wait and work for Him. Hand and heart are His!

The Shulamite and her beloved *relish, too, love's strength:* "For love is strong as death" (8:6a). The believer has many enemies in life, the last and the worst of which is death. And death is an enemy, the Bible says so. It is, however, the last enemy and, as C. H. Spurgeon used to say, "Since death is the last enemy we best leave him till last."

Note *what they realized.* Mention is made of *the vindictiveness they expected:* "Jealousy is cruel as the grave: the coals thereof are coals of fire, which hath a most vehement flame" (8:6b). Envy and jealousy are not rational passions.

They are white-hot emotions set on fire of hell itself. But revenge is foolish and futile.

When Solomon wrote Ecclesiastes, he told how hopeless and unsatisfying had been his wild fling along those lines: "I applied mine heart . . . to know the wickedness of folly, even of foolishness and madness: And I find more bitter than death the woman, whose heart is snares and nets, and her hands as bands: whoso pleaseth God shall escape from her; but the sinner shall be taken by her. Behold, this have I found, saith the Preacher, counting one by one, to find out the account; Which yet my soul seeketh, but I find not: one man among a thousand have I found; but a woman among all those have I not found" (Ecclesiastes 7:25-28). The Shulamite, of course, was not numbered in that thousand.

The Bible reveals that once the Church is taken away, at the rapture, and placed in the safekeeping of the Shepherd beyond Satan's reach, forever thwarted in his efforts to despoil her, Satan will vent his rage elsewhere.

The Church will cleave the sky, Heaven-born and Heaven-bound. Then Satan will be cast down and here is the result: "Therefore rejoice, ye heavens, and ye that dwell in them. Woe to the inhabiters of the earth and of the sea! for the devil is come down unto you, having great wrath, because he knoweth that he hath but a short time" (Revelation 12:12). What a picture! Satan, in a jealous rage because the Church has taken over in the heavenlies, where for so long he himself held undisputed sway as "prince of the power of the air," is confined now to the environs of earth, the very place where for so long he attempted to tamper with the Church. Thus restricted, Satan will vent his spite on Israel in particular and on mankind in general. Vindictiveness is to be expected after the rapture of the Church.

The Shulamite and the shepherd speak now of *the victory they experienced:* "Many waters cannot quench love, neither can the floods drown it: if a man would give all the substance of his house for love, it would utterly be contemned" (8:7).

Love is what it is all about! Love it was that drew our Beloved down from the skies, love it was that took Him to Calvary, and on down into the regions of death. His was love, invincible love, the love that many waters cannot quench, that the floods can never drown. Love wins out in the end. After the rapture of the Church, Satan will persecute the woman, the nation of Israel: "And when the dragon saw that he was cast unto the earth, he persecuted the woman which brought forth the man child. . . . And the serpent cast out of his mouth water as a flood after the woman, that he might cause her to be carried away of the flood. And the earth helped the woman, and the earth opened her mouth, and swallowed up the flood which the dragon cast out of his mouth" (Revelation 12:13-16). Satan's malice, envy, and rage will not accomplish anything in the end. All he will succeed in doing is to further the sovereign purposes of God. Love will triumph at last.

B. The Shulamite and Her Brothers (8:8-12)

The brothers of the Shulamite are introduced three times into the Song of Solomon (1:6; 2:15; 8:8). They repressed the Shulamite, were harsh toward her, and did all they could to hinder her love for the shepherd. They made her the keeper of the vineyard. The brothers represent the nation of Israel. The Shulamite describes them as "my mother's children." She does not actually call them her brothers but rather uses an expression which, while it denotes nearness of kin, suggests estrangement and distance. They are not her beloved brothers; they are her mother's children.

Israel and the Church are near of kin, for both were brought into the world by God. They have much in common. They speak the same language of faith. They revere the same heroes of the past, owe much to a common body of inspired Biblical truth, and tread a not dissimilar path. Chosen and elected, as both undoubtedly were, there is distance between them. The Shulamite and her brothers quarreled over her love for the shepherd. The parting of the roads between Israel and the Church is over the self-same issue—the Shepherd, the person of Christ. Israel has no use for Jesus; the Church has given Him her all. Thus, although Israel and the Church have much in common, they have an issue between them which is vital, fundamental, and significant.

The Shulamite describes the task to which she was sent: "They made me keeper of the vineyards." Three trees in the Bible symbolize the nation of Israel: the olive, the fig, and the vine. The fig symbolizes Israel as she is today—a nation of a Christ-rejecting character. The Lord gave his disciples the sign of His coming again: the fig tree would once again put forth its leaves and this coming revival of the fig tree would herald the approaching end of the age.

The corporate life of the nation of Israel came to an end in A.D. 70, when the Romans sacked Jerusalem, burned the Temple, and slew or enslaved or deported the mass of the people. From then until recent times the Jewish people existed without a state of their own. Then in 1948 the nation came back to life and several million Jews once more reside in the land. The nation has put forth its leaves. Israel is just as it was when Christ withdrew His blessing centuries ago—a Christ-rejecting, religious nation without any knowledge of the Shepherd.

The olive, on the other hand, anticipates a day which has not yet dawned, a day when the Jews will own Christ as their long-rejected Messiah. Once again Israel will have that spiritual ascendancy and privilege over the nations, taken away from them for their crucifixion of Christ and persecution of the Church. Romans 11 makes it clear that God intends to graft the nation of Israel back into the olive tree from which it was broken off. That will not take place until the nation of Israel has been purged in the fires of the great tribulation.

The vine represents Israel throughout its Old Testament history. It was a vine that Israel was uprooted from Egypt, carried across the sands of Sinai, and rooted and planted in the promised land of Canaan. It was as a vine that Israel brought forth sour grapes. It was as a vine that Israel resisted all the attempts of the great Husbandman to improve it. It was as a vine that Israel's wickedness and stubbornness came to a head: the keepers of the vineyard, the elders and leaders of the nation, maltreated those sent to them by God and crowned all their other sins by murdering the Owner's beloved Son.

The Lord Jesus had all this in view when he announced not only that the vineyard would be taken away from Israel and given to someone else, but also that from henceforth He was to be regarded as the true Vine.

When the Shulamite says that her brothers made her the "keeper of the vineyard" we can see where the typology leads. It was not her own vineyard she was to keep, it was theirs. Similarly, Israel's miserable failure made it necessary for their spiritual privileges and responsibilities to be transferred to somebody else who would be faithful in the task of keeping the vineyard for God.

"My mother's children were angry with me," the Shulamite describes her relationship to those who should have been the most sympathetic to her.

The early Church met in the home of Jews, the disciples and apostles were all Jews, and kept the Jewish forms of faith. The Jewish Christian believers frequented the temple services, observed Jewish vows and forms, sought coexistence with the ancestral faith. They did not seek or desire any break with the past, with the comfortable family life of the Hebrew faith. It was not long, however, before the issue of the Shepherd led to friction. The Jews as a nation resented and rejected the Lord Jesus Christ and became angry with those who proclaimed their love for Him. The official attitude of the nation of Israel hardened into one of repression and hostility. It did not take long for the real point of controversy to surface. The Sanhedrin summoned Peter and John and "commanded them not to speak at all nor teach in the name of Jesus" (Acts 4:18).

The Shulamite's brothers not only put her in the vineyard, they ridiculed her by giving her what seemed an impossible task: "Take us the foxes, the little foxes, that spoil the vines" (2:15). Foxes are noted for their craft and cunning. How could the Shulamite hope to catch foxes? It was a hopeless and thankless task of outwitting a clever, cruel foe.

It is significant, surely, that the Lord Jesus called only one of His foes, Herod Antipas, a man dubbed by even secular historians as "a wily sneak," a fox (Luke 13:32). This was the man who murdered John and who mocked at Jesus.

It is also significant that the early Church had to face the hatred of another Herod, Herod Agrippa I. Like all his kin he, too, was an unscrupulous, cruel fox of a man, who executed James and incarcerated Peter. God made a signal example of Agrippa when he snapped at the Church. Before his day was done God smote him for his brutality and blasphemy and sent a worm to gnaw at his living flesh with all the horrors of the tomb.

Now the Shulamite's brothers respect her (8:8). The long days of estrangement and separation are over. The Shulamite has proved herself and the shepherd has come at last to claim his beloved. The brothers give in, won over as well.

Thus, too, it will be in a coming day. The nation of Israel will be reconciled with the Church of God. After the coming of the great Shepherd, after the Church has been taken to be with Him, when the Lord comes with His bride— then Israel will see at long last how wrong she has been and how right the Church was in her love for Christ.

In the closing stanzas of this song the brothers make *an assessment* of the Shulamite: "We have a little sister, and she hath no breasts: what shall we do for our sister in the day when she shall be spoken for?" (8:8) Note *what they perceived:* their sister is immature, they cannot get used to the idea that she has grown up.

As men of the world look at the Church they see it as a little thing, without maturity. They scorn it because their viewpoint is prejudiced and distorted, confusing Christendom with the Church, the outward and apparent for the inward and real. However, down through the centuries, in times of testing and trial, in times of peace and prosperity, the true Church has been growing and developing, and will soon be ready for the rapture and the bridal song.

Note what the Shulamite's brothers *proposed:* "If she be a wall, we will build upon her a palace of silver" (8:9a). A wall symbolizes *invincibility.* How has our sister reacted during her enforced stay in Solomon's court? Has she withstood the temptations with which she has been faced? If so, "We will build upon her a palace," or as Rotherham renders it, "If a wall she is we will build upon it a battlement of silver." Her brothers had misunderstood and maligned her in the past but, if she came through this examination with flying colors, they would give her the place that was rightfully hers.

"If she be a door, we will inclose her with boards of cedar" (8:9b). A door is a symbol of *invitation*. An open door says, "Come in," and even a closed door can be forced. In ancient cities the weak point in the defenses was the door or the gate which gave access to the city. This was always the point where the enemy brought up his battering rams and artillery. "Has our sister been open to Solomon's proposals?" If so, then they proposed a prison.

The whole scene is a kind of judgment seat before which their little sister was summoned and arraigned and tried. And there is a judgment seat for the Church. We do not know all who will be there, but we do know we will, and the Lord will be there. It will be a time of investigation and testing when the deeds done in the body will be examined and explained. The true Church, as made up of its members, will have to appear and give answer. Not that we need to have any qualms about the outcome. There is no prison for us, only a palace.

If we have an assessment in verse 9, we have *an assertion* in verses 10-12. The Shulamite bears radiant testimony to the way she behaved in the hands of the tempter in his palace. How thankful she is now that she defied and defeated him.

We note the Shulamite's *testimony:* "I am a wall, and my breasts like towers: then was I in his eyes as one that found favor" (8:10). She likens her impregnability to a castle wall, strong, guarded by towers. She could look her brothers in the eye and assert her purity. Her beloved was satisfied, what grounds had they for criticism or complaint?

That, of course, is going to be the end result of the judgment seat of Christ. It is not a mercy seat but a judgment seat. Our lives will be brought into review and our works will be tested by fire. Whatever is of wood, hay, or stubble will be burned up, and out of the fiery trial will come the gold, the silver, the precious stones. Calvary has taken care of all the rest. Our faults and failings, that which we have done in the flesh, our unconfessed sins, our shameful downfalls, all this will be between us and our Lord alone, and Calvary will be found to have covered it all. The very memory of such things will vanish like smoke before a driving wind.

Out of the fire will appear those precious things, born of the Spirit of God. All that will ever be seen of the earthly will be the things which bring joy and delight to the heart of God. The Church will stand forth a glorious Church, without spot or wrinkle or any such thing, arrayed in the fine linen of the righteousness of saints. It will be presented flawless, impeccable, and perfect before God, before Israel and before the world. The Church of God, as the Lord Jesus has always seen it, will be displayed mighty, mature, marriageable.

The Shulamite told of *her triumph:* "Solomon had a vineyard at Baal-hamon; he let out the vineyard unto keepers; every one for the fruit thereof was to bring a thousand pieces of silver. My vineyard, which is mine, is before me: thou, O Solomon, must have a thousand, and those that keep the fruit thereof two hundred" (8:11-12). This may be paraphrased, "A vineyard had Solomon as the owner of abundance, he put out the vineyard to keepers—every man was to bring in, for the fruit thereof, a thousand silverlings: mine own vineyard is before me—the thousand belong to thee O Solomon, and two hundred to the keepers of the fruit thereof" (Rotherham).

That's the way to talk to the enemy! Take a hard look at all his property and power, look well at all he has to offer, at all his hired servants, at all his wealth and means, and say: "Keep it!"

The name Baal-hamon means "lord of the multitude." There is no doubt that the crowds flocked to Solomon, impressed by what he had to offer. The masses will always settle for less than the best. Not the Shulamite!

The number two hundred is used in Scripture to highlight the thought of insufficiency. When Jesus challenged His disciples to feed the five thousand, Philip said, "Two hundred pennyworth of bread is not sufficient." What the prince of this world has to offer is never sufficient, it always falls short of expectations, it never satisfies. Satan can never bring lasting satisfaction to an empty, craving, longing human heart. God has engineered the human soul for eternity. He has so shaped and fashioned it that it can be satisfied with nothing less than Himself. Satan's strategy is to focus our attention on this world where he is prince. God would have us focus on that world where the Shepherd is all in all.

C. THE SHULAMITE AND HER BETROTHED (8:13-14)

There are others who might well belong in this closing picture, but they fade into the background. The Shulamite and the shepherd only have eyes and ears for each other. We note *the shepherd's last request:* "Thou that dwellest in the gardens, the companions hearken to thy voice: cause me to hear it." The story ends appropriately in a garden. Paradise has been regained. The shepherd uses a word for "dwellest" which literally means to "abide permanently." Never again will his beloved be in peril from the world or its prince. She has come into his garden at last, there to remain in a paradise of bliss forever. He has no higher hope of happiness than to hear her voice. Whatever can she say to him? She can tell him again and again, "I love you, I love you, I love you." That is all the music he desires.

The Shepherd, the Lord Jesus Christ, the uncreated, eternal Son of the living God, He who has had the shining seraphim to be His slaves, who fills all Heaven with His praise—*He* says to *us*, "Cause Me to hear thy voice." Can thoughts soar higher than this?

He has so arranged the ages that, at last, He will bring us into a Paradise much fairer than that which He planted eastward in Eden. There He will say to us, "Now then, let Me hear thy voice." We cannot explain it, we cannot enter into it, we can hardly believe it! We borrow the language of the psalmist and say, "Such knowledge is too wonderful for me, it is too high."

He longs to hear our voices even today. He loves to hear them raised in songs of adoration and praise. He loves to hear our words of worship. But what can we possibly say to Him, to Him whose word can create stars and suns?

> Take my love; my Lord I pour
>   At Thy feet its treasure store.
> Take myself and I will be
>   Ever, only, all for Thee.
>   FRANCES RIDLEY HAVERGAL

We have the shepherd's last request: "Cause me to hear thy voice! Tell me you love me!"

Then comes *the Shulamite's last reply:* "Make haste, my beloved, and be thou like to a roe or to a young hart upon the mountains of spices" (8:14). She no longer talks about the mountains of separation (2:17)—those are of the past; she talks about the mountains of spices—"the scented slopes" is Moffatt's picturesque rendering.

What would our Shepherd want us to say to Him that could exceed that? Why, nothing at all! "Lord Jesus, come! Come in all Your vigor and in the splendor of that bound-less life of Yours! Come! Leap over all obstacles! Let nothing ever come between us again, even the most pleasant things we could imagine, mountains of spices, let nothing ever come between us again!"

The love song ends where the book of Revelation ends, where the Bible itself ends: "Even so, come, Lord Jesus!"